THE 10 MOST COMMON CHESS MISTAKES

...and how to avoid them!

THE 10 MOST COMMON CHESS MISTAKES

...and how to avoid them!

Larry Evans

CARDOZA PUBLISHING

ABOUT THE AUTHOR

Grandmaster Larry Evans, one of America's most celebrated chess authorities, is a 5-time USA champion and author of more than 20 chess books including *New Ideas in Chess, Chess Catechism, Modern Chess Brilliancies*, and a collaboration on Bobby Fischer's classic *My 60 Memorable Games*. He is a longtime contributor to *Chess Life*, and his syndicated chess column, *Evans On Chess*, has appeared continuously since 1971. Evans has beaten or drawn games against six world champions: Euwe, Karpov, Petrosian, Spassky, Smyslov, and Fischer, as well as dozens of the worlds' top players.

Evans first won the Marshall Club Championship at 15 and the New York State Championship at 16. He won the USA Closed Championship five times (the first time in 1951, the last time in 1980–a remarkable span), the USA Open four times, the 1956 Canadian Open, as well as many opens over the years including first place at an international tournament in Portugal 1974. Evans represented the USA on eight Olympic teams (including the gold medal team in 1976) and served as captain in 1982.

Evans was the youngest player to capture the nation's highest chess title at age 19, a record surpassed only by Bobby Fischer at 14. He is sometimes referred to as the dean of American chess.

FIRST EDITION

Library of Congress: 98-71036
ISBN: 1-58042-009-5

CARDOZA PUBLISHING

PO Box 1500, Cooper Station, New York NY 10276
Phone (718)743-5229 • Fax (718)743-8284
Email: Cardozapub@aol.com
Web Site: www.cardozapub.com

Write for your free catalogue of gaming and chess books, equipment, software and computer games.

TABLE OF CONTENTS

INTRODUCTION

"The mistakes are all there, waiting to be made."
Savielly Tartakower

This fascinating collection of 218 errors, misplays, oversights, and outright blunders, will not only show you the price that great players pay for violating basic principles, but how you can avoid these mistakes in your own game. You'll be challenged to choose between two moves; the right one, or the one actually played in the game. You'll learn the thinking and strategic concepts behind the correct play, where the game was heading, and often, what the players were actually thinking when the decisive move was made!

From neglecting development, king safety, misjudging threats, and premature attacks, to impulsiveness, snatching pawns, and basic inattention, you will get a complete course in exactly where you can go wrong and how to fix it.

A perfect game will end in a draw and is apt to be dull. Yet few draws are perfect. Chess is fraught with mistakes. Nobody can win unless somebody makes a mistake. It's been said many times that the victor is he who makes the next-to-the-last mistake.

Bad moves come in all shapes and sizes, from simple oversights to hideous blunders. They are usually caused by inexperience, lack of skill or just plain fatigue. To rule out time pressure as the culprit, I selected examples where both players had enough time on the clock to make rational choices.

The purpose of this book is to analyze how these mistakes were made and why they were made. Many of the illustrations were culled from my own games, and I was just as often the victim as the victor. Each diagram contains a choice between the right move or the one chosen in the actual game. I isolated ten different themes which often overlap, and the format enables you to match wits with the masters.

This compendium of incredible goofs by the world's best players could be subtitled "What's The Worst Move?" To err is human, but chess is unforgiving. You can't afford any lapses in concentration from first move to last. Despite 39 strong moves a single mistake on move 40 can wreck hours of hard work and cost the game.

In his heyday world champion Alexander Alekhine extolled the value of concentration: "One feature above all determines the strength of a chessplayer, the undivided attention which must absolutely isolate the player from the outside world."

Theory Of The Second Chance
There's an old saying that the hardest game to win is a won game. Not how to get it, but how to win it! The only thing harder than winning a won game is saving a lost one. Even world champions have thrown in the towel too soon.

When your position is bad, fight harder! In half a century of tournament experience I saved many hopeless games by just hanging in there and offering the stiffest possible resistance. I learned early on that no matter how bad things seem, there usually comes a point where you might salvage a draw or snatch victory from the jaws of defeat. These minor miracles occur for the simple reason that many opponents become increasingly uncertain when faced with stubborn opposition.

In 1926 Emanuel Lasker wrote: "He who has a slight disadvantage plays more attentively, inventively and more boldly than his antagonist who either takes it easy or aspires after too much. Thus a slight disadvantage is very frequently seen to convert into a good, solid advantage."

I call Lasker's insight "the theory of the second chance."

The Inner Game

Garry Kasparov became the youngest world champion at age 22. Yet despite all his formidable achievements over the board, he might be remembered 100 years from now solely as the strongest player who ever lost to a computer. Unlike us, machines don't tire or falter. The finale of their second game — a celebrated example of premature resignation — reflected his failure of will.

DEEP BLUE - KASPAROV
New York, 1997

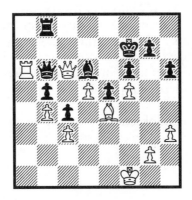

1. Black moves
(a) Qxc6 (b) Qe3

Kasparov was leading by a point going into this second game of a six game match when, demoralized by the machine's boa constrictor grip, he baffled spectators by resigning in a position that was later found to be drawn!

(a) Clearly there was no hope in 1...Qxc6 (or 1...Qd8; 2.Ra7+ Kg8; 3.Rd7) 2.dxc6 Rc8; 3.Ra7+ Rc7; 4.Ra8 and Black is hogtied.

(b) Kasparov rejected 1...Qe3! because, in his mind's eye, he saw 2.Qxd6 Qxe4; 3.Ra7+ Kg8; 4.Qxb8+ Kh7; 5.Ra1 Qf4+; 6.Kg1 Qe3+; 7.Kh1 and the king escapes by ducking into the corner.

But surely he had nothing to lose by first playing 1...Qe3! and then taking a long look at the position. He might have found the saving resource 2.Qxd6 Re8!! leading to a draw. One possible variation is 3. Bf3 (if 3. h4! h5! changes nothing) 3...Qc1+; 4.Kf2 Qd2+; 5.Be2 Qf4+; 6.Ke1 Qc1+; 7.Bd1 Qxc3+!; 8.Kf1 Qc1! and White's king can't wriggle out of perpetual check.

This kind of mistake comes under the heading of seeing ahead — but not far enough. The missed opportunity left an emotional scar from which Kasparov never recovered. He didn't win another game and went on to drop the match 3 1/2 - 2 1/2, a milestone that made headlines around the world.

Improving Your Game
Experience, said Oscar Wilde, is the record of our own mistakes. In order to determine your strong and weak points save all your scoresheets and review them in the future with a master or a stronger player. Write down your thoughts immediately after a game while they are still fresh and you will be surprised at how quickly your play improves.

Here's hoping this book enables you never to make the same mistake once.

Larry Evans
c/o Chesstours
Box 1182
Reno, Nevada 89504

Chapter 1

BAD DEVELOPMENT

"Help your pieces so that they can help you." — Paul Morphy

A good chess game, like a good yarn, has an opening, middle and end. The opening is a fight for time, territory and material. The first dozen moves or so are a prelude to the battle that lies ahead. Your main task is to emerge from the opening alive, especially when playing Black.

He who mobilizes all his reserves and gets to the scene of action "fustest with the mostest" is likely to secure an advantage in time and space. Often this is decisive if it can be transformed into material gain or a mating attack.

In chess as in life there are general guidelines but no eternal rules. Bearing in mind that each position must be evaluated on its own merits, the following tips gleaned from over a century of tournament experience should prove helpful.

GENERAL PRINCIPLES
1. Play to dominate the middle of the board. Occupy, attack or watch the center; the sides and corners are lifeless.

2. The opening is a race for rapid and continuous development. Develop all your men fast, not just one or two. Aim to connect rooks on the back rank so they can occupy central files.

3. Seize open lines!

4. Don't lose time by moving the same piece twice.

5. Avoid early queen sorties.

6. Develop knights before bishops. The course of the game usually suggests the best posts for bishops whereas knights generally belong on f3 and c3 (or c6 and f6 for Black).

7. Just move enough center pawns to free your forces on the back row. Bring out your bishops before hemming them in with pawns.

8. Castle early. This brings the king to safey and activates a rook towards the center.

9. Avoid useless checks.

10. Avoid cramped positions — they bear the germs of defeat. When cramped, try and swap pieces to get some elbow room.

INVITATION TO A BEHEADING

Just bringing out the pieces isn't good enough. You have to bring them to the right squares and consider what happens once they get there. Here Black wants to castle but must first decide on which of four squares to post his king's bishop.

EVANS - PEEBLES
New York, 1947

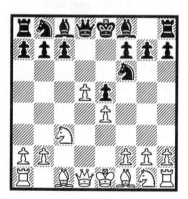

2. Black moves
(a) Bb4   (b) Bc5

(a) Black selected the worst possible place where the bishop was beheaded after 1...Bb4?; 2.Qa4+. He overlooked this double attack, known to the trade as a *fork*, and resigned on the spot.

(b) Where the bishop goes is largely determined by your style. Most players would rule out 1...Be7 because 2.Nf3 Nbd7 looks like a cramped and unpleasant way to defend the pawn on e5. 1...Bd6 is certainly solid, but somewhat passive, and could create problems later after Bg5 with an annoying pin.

Today I'd select 1...Bc5 without giving it too much thought. The bishop secures an active post and strikes at the vulnerable f2 square. This may not seem important, but White already must exercise care. For example, 2.Nf3? Ng4! can be nasty.

BACK RANK BLUES
White's only problem is his inactive knight on b1. But that's no reason to abandon ship.

BEDNARSKY - EVANS
Lugano Olympiad, 1968

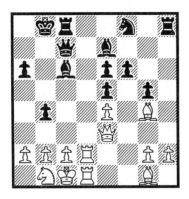

3. White moves
(a) h3 (b) c4

(a) A good plan is 1.h3 to free the bishop from the onerous task of defending the pawn on h2. Chances are roughly equal.

(b) Instead White got spooked by the pressure along the c-file and played 1. c4? hoping to continue with b3. He totally overlooked 1...Bxe4!; 2.Qxe4 Qxc4+; 3.Qxc4 Rxc4+; 4.Rc2 Rxg4 and suddenly I was two pawns up with an easy win in sight.

BIDING YOUR TIME
Even if you can't see how to strengthen your position, don't help your opponent improve his. A case in point.

FULLER - EVANS
Hastings, 1949/50

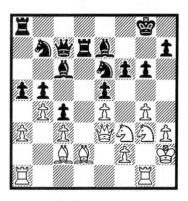

4. White moves
(a) Qh6 (b) Rad1

(a) Invading with 1.Qh6 is full of sound and fury, signifying nothing. In point of fact it merely lost time after 1...Bf8; 2.Qe3 (certainly not 2.Qh4? g5; 3.Qh5 Rxd2; 4.Nxd2 Be8 snaring the queen) 2...Rad8; 3.Rad1 Nf4 seizing the initiative.

(b) Since the action is shaping up on the open d-file, White should bide his time and start contesting it now with 1.Rad1 Rad8; 2.Bc1 with even chances.

MEANINGLESS THREATS
It bears repeating that you should avoid making threats that ignore development and help improve your opponent's position. Whatever possessed me to do such a thing? I plead youth and inexperience in my early days at the Marshall Club in Manhattan, when I was just a woodpusher.

GASSEN - EVANS
New York, 1946

5. Black Moves
(a) Ndf6 (b) Bg5

(a) The solid 1...Ndf6 strengthens the kingside and bolsters the knight on d5.

(b) What did I have in mind with 1...Bg5 attacking the rook? This silly sortie allowed White to assume the initiative by 2. Nxg5 Qxg5; 3.Ne4 Qd8; 4.Nd6.

WASTED MOVES
Every move is precious. Your main task is to reach a playable middle game without wasting time or dropping material.

SIMS - EVANS
San Diego Open, 1965

6. White moves
(a) 0-0 (b) Qd3

(a) In the absence of anything better, White should simply castle to rescue his king from the center while waiting to see where his other pieces should go. There's little to fear from doubled pawns resulting from 1.0-0 Bxc3; 2.bxc3 Ne5; 3.Ba3 Re8; 4.Qd4.

(b) Worried about Bxc3, White brought his queen out too early by 1.Qd3? which cost a pawn after 1...Ne5!; 2.Qc2 Nxc4; 3.0-0 (too late!) 3...d5 and I already had a technically won game.

WATCH THE CENTER
This arises from the Dragon Variation of the Sicilian Defense: l.e4 c5; 2.Nf3 Nc6; 3.d4 cxd4; 4.Nxd4 g6; 5.Nc3 Bg7; 6.Be3 Nf6; 7.Bc4 0-0; 8.Bb3. Now should Black put his knight on the rim to chase the bishop or open lines for his queen's bishop?

FISCHER - RESHEVSKY
USA Championship, 1958

7. Black moves
(a) Na5 (b) d6

(a) 1...Na5? is suspect because it decentralizes a knight and also violates principle by moving the same piece twice in the opening. Fischer, who avidly studied Russian chess literature, was familiar with a game just played in the USSR that White won after 2.e5! Nxb3 (if 2...Nh5 3 g4 traps this piece) 3.exf6 Nxa1; 4.fxg7. Reshevsky retreated 2...Ne8 and was stunned by 3.Bxf7+! Kxf7; 4.Ne6!! dxe6 (if 4...Kxe6; 5.Qd5+ Kf5; 6.g4+ Kxg4; 7.Rg1 mates in a few moves) 5.Qxd8. White won.

(b) Instead of relinquishing the guard on e5 Black should venti-
late a diagonal for his bishop with 1...d6.

TRYING FOR TOO MUCH TOO SOON

White has a lead in development and threatens Rxd7. In addition, Black must contend with how to get his king out of the
center. He ignored both of these problems and came to grief
by making a premature threat of his own.

DZINDZIHASHVILI - LUBOYEVIC
26th Olympiad, 1984

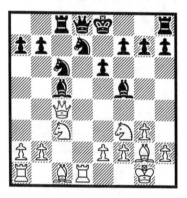

8. Black moves
(a) Qe7 (b) Nb4

(a) Black can make a start towards solving his problems with
the prudent 1...Qe7 intending Nb6 and then castling. Too rash
is 1...Qb6; 2.Na4! Bxf2+; 3.Kf1.

(b) Instead Black moved a developed piece again by 1...Nb4?
with the crude threat of Bxf2+ and the secondary idea of Nc2.
This met with swift retribution by 2.Be3! Be7 (too risky is
2...Bxe3; 3.Qxb4 Qb6; 4.Qa4 Bxf2+; 5.Kf1 Rd8; 6.Rxd7! Rxd7;
7.Ne5 with a devastating pin; also inferior is 2...Nc2; 3.Bxc5
Nxa1; 4.Rxd7! Qxd7; 5.Ne5 Qc7; 6.Qb5+ Kd8; 7.Bd6 Qxd6;
8.Nxf7+ Ke7; 9.Nxd6) 3.Qf4 Nc2; 4.Ne5 Nxa1; 5.Rxd7 Qa5;
6.Rxb7 Qa6; 7.Rxa7 Qd6; 8.Qa4+ Kf8; 9.Bf4 and Black resigns
because there's no good defense to Nd7+.

TACTICAL TRICKS

Material is even but Black actually has more pieces out than White, who still has three minor pieces stranded on the back rank. The obvious 1.Bb5+ leads to nought after 1...Bd7. So White must seek something forceful to overcome his lag in development.

KASHDAN - TARTAKOWER
London, 1932

9. White moves
(a) Bh6   (b) Qxf6

(a) A more or less stock combination to gain the exchange is 1.Bh6! which serves four purposes: 1. It brings out a fresh piece. 2. It defends the queen. 3. It threatens Qf8+. 4. It amasses material after either 1...Qxh6; 2.Qxh8 or 1...Ng6; 2.Qxf6 Nxf6; 3.Bg7. If Black tries to get cute with 1...Ng4, then 2.Qf8+ Kd7; 3.Bb5+ Kc7; 4.Qc5+ Kd8; 5.Qd6+ Bd7; 6.Qxd7 mate.

(b) There are precious few second chances. After the lame 1.Qxf6? Nxf6, Black managed to escape with a draw.

OPEN FILES

We are accustomed to think of lack of development as a bunch of pieces snoozing on the back row, but it can take other forms as shown here. An exchange up, Black has every expectation of winning but must exercise care to avoid a draw by three-move repetition inasmuch as the same position already was reached twice before.

WINTER - MILNER BARRY
London, 1932

10. Black moves
(a) Qa1+ (b) Rb8

(a) After 1...Qa1+; 2.Rd1 Qe5; 3.Rd5 White, who is behind in material, gladly claimed a draw by repetition.

(b) Since Black's rook is not needed on d8, he can improve its power by seizing the open file with 1...Rb8! which, incidentally, neuters 2.Rxe5? Rb1. It also avoids the danger of a draw by repetition by changing the position.

In his notes Alekhine pointed out the following variation to exploit the weakness of White's back rank: 1...Rb8!; 2.g3 (2.Rd1 is better but in the long run Black's material superiority would prevail) 2...Rxg3!; 3.hxg3 Qxg3; 4.Rd3 Rb1+; 5.Bd1 Rxd1+; 6.Rxd1 Qf3+; 7.Kh2 Qxd1; 8.Qf7+ Kb6; 9.Qxh7 Qxa4 with an easy win.

DESPERADO

Desperado is a term applied to a piece that inevitably is bound to be lost but, before being captured, causes as much damage as possible. Here Black didn't bother to calculate with care before making what seemed to be a sound positional move.

EUWE - COLLE
Carlsbad, 1929

11. Black moves
(a) e5 (b) Qe7

(a) Black simply forgot about the danger lurking on the long diagonal and dropped a pawn by 1...e5?; 2.Nxe5! Bxg2 (no better is 2...dxe5; 3.Bxb7 Rb8; 4.dxe5!) 3.Nxd7 Bh3? (he should settle for 3...Qxd7) 4.Nxf8 Black Resigns.

(b) A normal game arises after 1...Qe7 to complete development by connecting rooks on the back rank.

WHITHER GOEST THOU?

As noted earlier, it's not enough just to bring out your pieces. You also must bring them to the right squares — a truism that even great players sometimes forget.

KARPOV - KASPAROV
7th match game, 1990

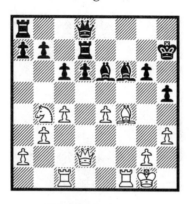

12. Black moves
(a) Qa5 (b) Qh8

(a) 1...Qa5? pins the knight to the queen, which is protected, so the knight is free to move. White won material and the game after 2.Nd5! Qc5+ (if 2...Qxd2; 3.Nxf6+ Kg7; 4 Bxd2 wins a piece; or 2...Qd8; 3.Nxf6+ Qxf6; 4.Bxd6 Qd8; 5.e5 gains a pawn with a bind) 3.Kh1 (avoiding the complications flowing from 3.Be3 Bg5) 3...Bxd5; 4.cxd5 Qd4; 5.dxc6 bxc6; 6 Rxc6.

(b) The strange-looking 1...Qh8! prepares to develop the queen's rook to e8. The pawn is untouchable since 2.Bxd6? Bd4+ snares a piece. Note also that the inactive rook on a8 is free to move to the center.

WRONG SQUARES

Karpov made fewer blunders and won more first prizes than any other world champion in history. This may well be the worst blunder of his career in a relatively pressure-free opening.

CHRISTIANSEN - KARPOV
Wijk aan Zee, 1993

13. Black moves
(a) Bd6 (b) Bc5

(a) 1...Bd6? makes perfect positional sense. It fights for control of the center and anticipates 2.Be2 Nf4 getting the knight back into play. Alas, White bagged a piece by switching back with 2.Qd1! setting up a double attack on the knight and bishop. Karpov resigned on the spot. Fans watching the game on the demo board talked about this blunder for the rest of the day.

(b) Probably the most active post for the bishop is on c5. 1...Bc5 would have enabled Karpov to avoid the shortest loss of his career.

SHORT TAKE
The shortest tournament game between two masters arose from the Budapest Defense: 1.d4 Nf6; 2.Nd2 e5!?; 3.dxe5 Ng4.

GIBAUD - LAZARD
Paris, 1924

14. White moves
(a) h3 (b) Ngf3

(a) This is a good illustration of how too many pawn pushes can quickly prove fatal. After 1.h3? Ne3! White resigned as he must either drop his queen or get mated after 2.fxe3 Qh4.

(b) It's a normal game after 4.Ngf3 Nc6, regaining the pawn.

CALLING A BLUFF

A grandmaster who had 40 years of experience and wrote more than 40 instructional manuals was once checkmated in 11 moves from the Caro-Kann Defense: 1.e4 c6; 2.d4 d5; 3.Nc3 dxe4; 4.Nxe4 Nf6; 5.Qd3 e5?!; 6.dxe5 Qa5+; 7.Bd2 Qxe5; 8 0-0-0.

RETI - TARTAKOWER
Vienna, 1910

15. Black moves
(a) Nxe4   (b) Be7

(a) Black thought White couldn't castle because it loses a piece. He called Reti's bluff with 8...Nxe4? (also bad is 8...Qxe4?; 9.Re1) but was stung by 9.Qd8+! Kxd8; 10.Bg5+ Kc7 (or 10...Ke8; 11.Rd8 mate) 11.Bd8 mate. This is probably the most famous example of a discovered double check.

(b) If Black had been more suspicious, he would have tried to get his pieces out by 8...Be7 and then castle as fast as possible.

FIGHTING CRAMPS

Material is even but Black's forces are hemmed in. He can sit back and wait or try to burst his bonds.

SPASSKY - PETROSIAN
21st match game 1969

16. Black moves
(a) Nxd3 (b) Bxd5

(a) Petrosian followed the old precept that the best way to relieve a cramp is to swap a few pieces. But after 1...Nxd3?; 2.Qxd3 Ba8; 3.Nc4 Nc5; 4.Bxc5 Rxc5; 5.Ra4 h6; 6.Qd2 Be7; 7.Rea1 Bb7; 8.Qxb4 f5; 9 Ra7 Black was in a bad way.

(b) Black should seize the chance to mix it up with 1...Bxd5!; 2.Bxc5 (or 2.exd5 e4; 3.Nxe4 Nxe4=) 2...Nxc5; 3.exd5 e4; 4.Bxe4 Bxa1; 5.Rxa1 f5; 6.Ng5 Qb7! with active counterplay. It's certainly better than the way he got ground down in the game.

NO EXIT

Black's position is unenviable but playable. Who could believe it would collapse in just two more moves?

PETROSIAN - MATANOVIC
USSR - Yugoslavia, 1969

17. Black moves
(a) Rad8 (b) Qf4

(a) Black should bring his rook into play by 1...Rad8 and hope for the best. He needn't worry about 2.g3 Qxh3. And he gets some counterplay against 2.Qe2 Nd6; 3.Bxd6 cxd6; 4.Qxa6 d5; 5.Ng3 e4.

(b) Instead after 1...Qf4?; 2.Qe2 (why not 2 Qh5! right away?) 2...Na5; 3.Qh5! Black resigned because the lady has no escape. If 3...f5; 4.g3 Qxe4; 5.Rxe4 fxe4 doesn't get enough for the queen.

LIGHT ARTILLERY

Conventional wisdom holds that you should bring out minor pieces (bishops and knights) before major pieces (rooks and queens). It's a good idea to keep the heavy artillery in reserve for later stages of the battle.

LAPANG - JENSSEN
Denmark, 1937

18. Black moves
(a) Qf6 (b) Nd7

(a) 1...Qf6? is tempting because it threatens Bxf3 wrecking the pawn structure but it's too soon for the queen to enter the fray. Black imagined that 2 Bg5 Bxf3 won a piece but 3.Qd2! Qxd4; 4.Bxh7+ Kxh7; 5.Qxd4 caught his queen instead.

(b) It's time to unleash the cavalry with 1...Nd7 and transfer the horse to the embattled kingside. There's no need to worry about 2.Bxh7+? Kxh7; 3.Ng5+ Kg8; 4.Qh5 Nf6.

ANTICIPATE

White's center is obviously under fire. Before moving the bishop from the back rank he should anticipate that Black's next move will be ...Nc6 putting more pressure on the advanced pawns.

SAMSA - KUDRIN
Chicago, 1997

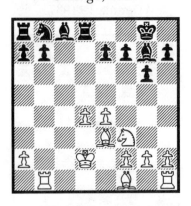

19. White moves
(a) Bc4   (b) Bd3

(a) White's must develop his bishop to its most effective post. He charged ahead with 1.Bc4? which, however, lost a vital tempo after 1...Nc6; 2.d5 Na5; 3.Bd3 e6 destroying the center and wresting the initiative.

(b) With a little foresight it's easy to see that White must fight to avoid a disadvantage with 1.Bd3 Nc6; 2.d5 Na5; 3.Ke2 b6; 4.Rhc1. Careless would be 1.Be2 Nc6; 2.d5 e6 again demolishing the center.

EXPECT THE UNEXPECTED

Alekhine's combinations were often startling because he searched for the unexpected and shunned routine moves. This policy may cost time on the clock, but it always pays to be alert.

YE RONGGUANG - VAN WELY
Antwerp, 1997

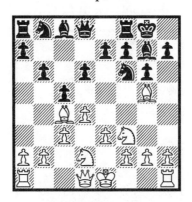

20. White moves
(a) Bxf6 (b) dxc5

(a) Ordinarily White should complete development with 1.0-0 but this is too routine. Although masters would never dream of swapping a bishop for knight without provocation, here is an exception to the rule because 1.Bxf6! Bxf6; 2.Bd5 wins a piece.

(b)After 1.dxc5? dxc5 the bishop no longer has access to d5. White missed a golden opportunity.

FRESH HORSES

Both sides are fully developed and rooks are connected on the back ranks, a sign that the middle game has arrived. Black is slightly worse because of his isolani at d5, but it does give him some breathing room.

PETROSIAN - SPASSKY
8th match game, 1969

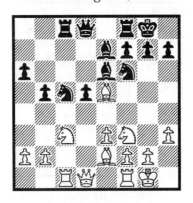

21. White moves
(a) Bd3 (b) Nd4

(a) White tried to improve his position by 1.Bd3? but met with a stern rebuke in 1...d4! which rid Black of his only weakness and gained the exchange after 2.Bxd4 Nxd3; 3.Qxd3 Bc4; 4.Qb1 Bxf1; 5.Rxf1 Nd5.

(b) It's time to bring out fresh horses with 1 Nd4. This maneuver not only stops ...d4 once and for all, but also carves out an excellent post for the bishop on f3.

Chapter 2

NEGLECTING THE KING

"Uneasy lies the head that wears a crown." —Shakespeare

The object of the game is checkmate, a word that derives from the Persian "shahmat" meaning the king (shah) is dead (mat).

Nothing is more important than safeguarding your king by castling early, within the first dozen moves if possible. It's the only time during a game that moving two pieces at once is allowed. Take advantage of this maneuver provided your king will be secure after you tuck it in.

Leaving the king in the center too long is the leading cause of disaster in the opening, even among top players. Castling too early, on the other hand, is far less dangerous.

"You castle your way. I'll castle my way." — George Treysman

On which side should you castle? It depends on the position, of course, but most players castle kingside because it's faster: only two pieces (bishop and knight) stand between the king and rook, whereas three pieces (bishop, knight, queen) must be cleared away to castle queenside. Here are some database statistics:

> White castles kingside — 80.2%
> White castles queenside — 8.8%
> White doesn't castle — 11%

Figures also show that White castled queenside nearly twice as much as Black. Both sides castling kingside is the norm, and this produces the highest draw percentages. The most decisive results occur when both players castle on opposite wings because of the imbalance created in the position.

Recently I received an interesting query for my Chess Life column from Karachi, Pakistan, about the need to castle when queens are off the board.

Q. A lively debate is afoot at the Mehran Chess Academy here about the importance of castling, especially in the absence of queens. One group is firmly in favor of castling — queens or no queens. The other side holds that the early exchange of queens renders castling quite unnecessary, arguing that once the distaff domination has disappeared the king stands better in the center where it lends much needed support to his officers and men. Would you favor us with your comments?

A. As a general rule the king is more effective near the center in the ending. The chief purpose of castling is to shield the king from attacks, but without queens on the board there is less to fear from enemy fire.

WHEN TO CASTLE
As a rule of thumb you should castle as soon as possible. But every rule has its exception.

EVANS - FISCHER
USA Championship 1965

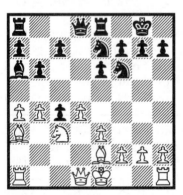

22. White moves
(a) 0-0 (b) b5

(a) White is a pawn down but I felt certain of regaining it at my leisure and carelessly chose 1.0-0? Ned5; 2.Rc1 c6!; 3.Bf3 b5 and Black held the pawn forever.

(b) It's necessary to delay castling for a move to regain the pawn by 1.b5 Bb7; 2.0-0. Now 2...Ned5 (not 2...Bd5; 3.f3 followed by e4) 3.Qc2 Nxc3; 4.Qxc3 Ne4; 5.Qc2 Qg5; 6.f4 (better than 6.Bf3 f5; 7.Qxc4 Nd2) 6...Qg6; 7.Bxc4 yields even chances.

WHEN NOT TO CASTLE

The main reason for delaying castling is that you can't be sure your king will be safe when it gets there. An equally valid reason is that there is something more important to do first.

EVANS - PILNICK
USA Championship, 1954

23. Black moves
(a) 0-0 (b) e6

(a) Black suffered for the rest of the game by remaining a pawn down after 1...0-0?; 2.Nf3 c6; 3.dxc6 Nxc6; 4.e3.

(b) Sometimes it's more important to regain the pawn and establish material equality than to castle. Necessary is 1...e6!; 2.Qd2 h6! 3.Nh3 exd5; 4.Qe3+ Kf8 and Black isn't in any great danger despite moving the king.

WEAKENED FORTRESS
Deciding where and when to castle is one of the most important decisions to make in the opening. A vital consideration is the integrity of the pawn structure surrounding the king's new abode.

PIKET - HERNANDEZ
Groningen, 1985

24. White moves
(a) 0-0 (b) Kf1

(a) Instead of using the pawn on h4 as the bulwark of a future attack, White made the dubious choice of 1.0-0!? placing the king on a weakened wing. This qualifies as an error of judgment rather than an outright error. More aggressive is 1.Qe2 or Qd2 followed by queenside castling.

(b) If White is determined not to risk queenside castling, then 1. Kf1 followed by 2.g3 and 3.Kg2 keeping the rook on h1 looks safer than the move chosen in the game.

WHICH WAY IS UP?

White can castle either way. Superficially, both look tempting, but one is flawed.

BARCZAY - UDOVIC
Zagreb, 1969

25. White moves
(a) 0-0 (b) 0-0-0

(a) The correct choice is 1.0-0 because the king is perfectly safe on that wing and White can later pile up against the backward pawn on d7 by Rad1.

(b) The problem with 1.0-0-0? is that it gives Black a target for his counterplay. Punishment was unusually swift after 1...Qa5; 2.Kb1 b5; 3.Bd3 c4; 4.Be4 Rb8; 5.Nd4 b4!; 6.Nxc6 dxc6; 7.cxb4 Bxb4 and White resigned (if 8.Qc1 Ba3; or 8.c3 Bxc3; finally 8.Qe2 Bc3; 9.Bc1 Bxb2; 10.Bxb2 Qc3).

WHAT, ME WORRY?

By now it's clear that there are essentially three reasons for not castling. (1) It's illegal. (2) You're not exactly sure if the king will be safe over there. (3) You have something more important to do first.

EVANS - FRENCH
New York, 1948

26. Black moves
(a) Bxc3 (b) 0-0

(a) It's generally not a good idea to swap a bishop for a knight without provocation. 1...Bxc3?; 2 Bxc3 0-0? (necessary is 2...Qc7; first; if 3.Bb4 a5 forces the bishop off the a3-f8 diagonal) 3.Bb4 Qc7; 4.Bxf8 and Black soon lost.

(b) Black must have been worried about something after 1...0-0 but what? If 2.e4?! Bxc3; 3.Bxc3 Nxe4; 4.Bb4 Nd6; 5.Bxd6 Qxd6; 6.Qxb7 Nd7 holds everything.

CASTLING INTO IT

In closed positions when the center is locked and a wall of pawns protects the king you have to think long and hard about where to castle. A premature decision can be very costly.

PACHMAN - GUIMARD
Prague, 1946

27. White moves
(a) c3 (b) 0-0

(a) Since c3 to bolster the pawn on d4 looks necessary sooner or later, it should be done before deciding on where to post the king. It's a good idea to wait until there is some indication of where will Black put his king.

(b) White made the mistake of committing himself too soon and lost quickly after 1.0-0? g5!; 2.g4 hxg4; 3.Bxg4 f5; 4.exf6 Nxf6; 5.h3 Nxg4; 6.hxg4 e5.

CASTLING OUT OF IT

Black is a pawn ahead but his king is stuck on the open e-file. Faced with the threat of Nd4 he has the unpleasant option to either move his king or castle, which appears to lose a piece.

GELLER - KERES
Zurich, 1953

28. Black moves
(a) Kf8 (b) 0-0

(a) If Black had nothing better, then 1...Kf8 would be the best defense even though White gets pressure for the pawn after 2.Bxc6 bxc6; 3 Bf4.

(b) Keres saw that 1...0-0; 2.Bxc6 bxc6; 3.Qxe7 loses a piece but he castled out of it anyway! The point of his little combination is 2.Bxc6 Bd6! — a pretty "zwischenzug," a German word meaning in-between move. By delaying the recapture until after White retreats his queen, Black solves his problems without worrying about any peril to his king. Geller retreated 2.Qe2 Re8 but lacked compensation for the pawn and eventually lost.

FIRST THINGS FIRST

What's the hurry? Always check to see if you have a better move before castling routinely.

CARLS - HEINRICH
Aachen, 1934

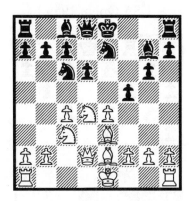

29. Black moves
(a) 0-0 (b) f4

(a) Black played the natural 1.0-0? and eventually lost the game.

(b) Black missed the immediate gain of a piece by 1...f4!; 2.Nxc6 fxe3; 3.Nxd8 exd2+; 4.Kxd2 Kxd8.

UGLY CHOICES

Sometimes an ugly move is necessary to avoid losing material even if it costs the right to castle. Neither choice is pretty, so just hold your nose and pick the lesser evil.

EVANS - RESHEVSKY
USA Open, 1955

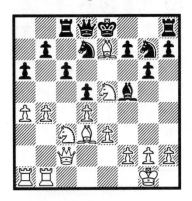

30. Black moves
(a) Qxe7 (b) Bxd3

(a) Black simply lost a pawn after 1...Qxe7?; 2.Nxd5. See also diagram 74 for a variation on this theme.

(b) Black can avoid losing a pawn by 1...Bxd3; 2.Nxd3 (better than 2.Qxd3 Qxe7) 2...Kxe7! After 3.b5 axb5; 4.axb5 Ne6 Black isn't sitting pretty, but it's better than giving up a button.

SENSING DANGER

Black is a pawn ahead and lags in development, but there doesn't appear to be any immediate danger. Or is there?

MEDNIS - EVANS
USA Championship, 1973

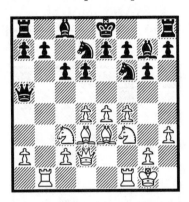

31. Black moves
(a) e5   (b) 0-0

(a) In order to prevent e5 Black made the mistake of fighting for control of the center with 1...e5? but overlooked 2.Nb5! Qxd2; 3.Nxd6+ Ke7; 4.Nxc8+ Rhxc8; 5 Bxd2. Suddenly White has regained the pawn with advantage.

(b) Castle first, philosophize later! After 1...0-0 there is nothing to fear from 2.e5 (if 2.Nd5 Qd8) 2...Ne8 remaining a solid pawn ahead. Eventually Black will wriggle out of the cramp and then can look forward to victory after consolidating.

WHAT'S THE HURRY?

The only excuse for not castling is if you have something more important to do. Again, first things first. This diagram arises from the Ruy Lopez: 1.e4 e5; 2.Nf3 Nc6; 3.Bb5 a6; 4.Ba4 Nf6; 5.0-0 Be7; 6.Qe2 b5; 7.Bb3 d6; 8.h3.

EVANS - MAGEE
1st USA Junior Championship
Chicago, 1946

32. Black moves
(a) Na5 (b) 0-0

(a) White's last move was inaccurate (better was c3 first in order to duck the bishop to c2.) Now 1...Na5! relieves the cramp and eliminates the bishop. Since there is no immediate danger, castling can be delayed for a move. 2.d4? cxd4; 3.Nxd4 c5; 4.Nf5 Bxf5; 5.exf5 c4 wins the bishop via the ancient Noah's Ark Trap.

(b) Black failed to avail himself of the opportunity to swap knight for bishop. The game continued 1...0-0; 2.c3 Na5; 3.Bc2 c5; 4.d4 Qc7 leading to standard lines in the Ruy Lopez.

DANGER AHEAD!
Black is already in trouble because he can't castle. He also faces the irritating threat of Qg7.

SEIRAWAN - IVANCHUK
Groningen, 1997

33. Black moves
(a) Qb6 (b) Qe7

(a) Black's queen is needed to defend the kingside but he made the strategical error of misplacing it on the other wing and got slaughtered after 1...Qb6?; 2.Bb1! Ke7 (if 2...Qxb2; 3.dxc6 bxc6; 4.Rxd6) 3.f4! exf4; 4.Rf1 Rf8; 5.Qxf4 f6; 6.dxc6 Qxc6; 7.Nd4 Qe8; 8.Nd5+ Kd8; 9.Qxd6+ Bd7; 10.Nb5. Black resigns.

(b) The best chance to survive is 1...Qe7; 2.Bb1 Bd7; 3.0-0 0-0-0 at least offering the king a semblance of safety.

STROLLING INTO MATE

Black's heavy pieces are massed on the queenside. Mate on the
other wing apparently was the last thing on his mind.

MASIC - MARIOTTI
Sombor, 1969

34. Black moves
(a) bxc4 (b) Kg7

(a) Black strolled into a forced mate after 1...bxc4?; 2 Nf5+! gxf5;
3.Rg1 and there is no defense to Rh3 (3...Nf6; 4.Rh3+ Nh5;
5.Rg5).

(b) There's no rush to do anything on the queenside. It's still a
hard game after 1...Kg7 safeguarding the king.

YOUR KING OR MINE?

White is a pawn ahead and his king looks secure despite the threat of Qc3 followed by Rd2. The time has come to get at Black's king, but how?

THOMAS - MITCHELL
London, 1932

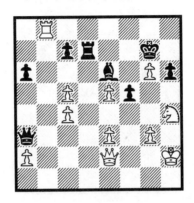

35. White moves
(a) Re8   (b) Qh5

(a) The winning line is 1.Re8! Qc3 (if 1...Bg8; 2.Nxf5+ Kxg6; 3.Qg4+ Kf7; 4.Qxg8 mate) 2.Rxe6 Rd2; 3.Nxf5+ Kf8; 4.g7+ Kf7; 5.Rf6+ Kd8; 6.g8/Q+ with fatal consequences.

(b) Instead Black actually lost after 1.Qh5? Qxa2+; 2.Kh3 Qf2; 3.Qf3 Qxf3; 4.Nxf3 f4+.

MORE BACK RANK WOES

Combinations often abound against the back rank when the king has no escape square. The best way to exploit this weakness isn't always apparent.

NAEGELI - GYGLI
Zurich, 1934

36. White moves
(a) Qxe5 (b) Qh5

(a) White made no attempt to trap the bishop on h2 and only drew after 1.Qxe5? Bxe5 because now 2.Rd8 Rb8 holds the back rank.

(b) White can win a piece by 1.Rd8 Rb8; 2.Rxb8 Qxb8; 3.g3 Bxg3; 4.fxg3 Qxg3 which looks messy. Cleaner is 1.Qh5! Rxe6; (if 1...Bxh5; 2.Rd8 mates; or 1...Rb8; 2.Qxh2) 2.Bxe6 Qxe6; 3.Rd8 g6; 4.Qxh2 Qe1+; 5.Qg1.

WHOSE KING IS WEAKER?

Players tend to get bolder when they believe their opponent is on the run. Here Black clearly has the initiative because his king on g8 appears stronger than its counterpart on e2.

GOLOMBEK - KOTTNAUER
Prague, 1946

37. Black moves
(a) Qg1 (b) g5

(a) White is hard-pressed after 1...Qg1 picking off the pawn on h2. Playing 2.Kf3 g5 increases the pressure on f4 and threatens g4+. Or 2.Qxc3 Qxh2+; 3.Ke3 Qg1+; 4.Ke2 h2 wins. Weaker is 1...Qb2; 2.Kd1.

(b) The tempting 1...g5?; 2 d4! creates an escape square on d3 and reveals Black's king as a vulnerable target. Play continued 2...Qh1; 3.Kd3 Qf3+; 4.Re3 Qxf4; 5.Qe2 Rd8; 6.Re4 Qc1; 7.Qg4! Qd2+; 8.Kc4 Rf8 (no better is 8...c2; 9.Qe6+ Kg7; 10.Qe7+) 9.Re5 c2; 10.Rxg5+ and Black resigns.

WHOSE KING IS SAFER?

Expect sharp play when both sides castle on opposite wings. Here Black would dearly love to pursue the attack by avoiding a queen swap yet he couldn't see far enough ahead.

MALEVINSKY - GEFENAS
Vilna, 1978

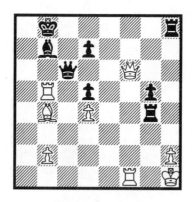

38. Black moves
(a) Rxh2+ (b) Qxf6

(a) Believe it or not, Black has a forced mate with 1...Rxh2+; 2.Kxh2 Qc2+!; 3.Qf2 Qh7+! But the idea of switching his queen to the kingside eluded him.

(b) Black rejected 1...Qxb5; 2.Qxh8+ Kh7; 3.Bc5+ Ka6; 4.Ra1+. Since he didn't see how to prosecute the attack, he settled for 1.Qxf6? Rxf6 and eventually lost.

SHATTERED FORTRESS

Often material must be sacrificed to breach the pawn wall around the enemy king. Then the only question is whether the defender has enough resources to beat back the attack.

PORTISCH - KARPOV
San Antonio, 1972

39. Black moves
(a) Kh8 (b) f5

(a) White gave up the exchange to shatter Black's kingside. The immediate threat is Rg4+ followed by Bd4. Karpov buckled under the pressure by 1...Kh8? overlooking 2.Rd5! and now there is no longer any defense if 2...Qxb2; 3.Bd4 Qc1+; 4.Kh2.

(b) It's arguable whether White even has enough compensation for the exchange after 1...f5!; 2.Rd5 Qxb2; 3.Bd4 Qb1+; 4.Kh2 f6!; 5.Rxf5 Qe4. Unfortunately, White was never put to the test.

A BRIDGE TOO FAR

Mikhail Tal briefly held the world championship in 1960 before losing a return match to Mikhail Botvinnik in 1961. Tal was considered the premier attacking player of modern times, yet he almost botched this one.

TAL - PEREZ
Havana, 1963

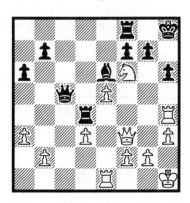

40. White moves
(a) Qe3 (b) Rh5

(a) Black has to give up his queen for a rook after 1.Qe3! because there is no other defense to 2.Rxh6+ gxh6; 3.Qxh6+. On 1...Rxh4; 2.Qxc5 is curtains.

(b) Instead Tal delayed a move by 1.Rh5? giving Black time to defend himself by 1...Rfd8; 2.Qe3 Qf8! Still oblivious to the threat, however, Perez returned the favor with 1.Rh5? Rc8?; 2.Qe3 and resigned in view of 2...Qf8; 3 Qxd4.

ASLEEP AT THE SWITCH

Sometimes we don't realize our kingside is weak until it's too late. Here I was a comfortable pawn up and never dreamed there was any danger.

PANDOLFINI - EVANS
National Open, 1970

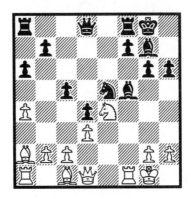

41. Black moves
(a) c4 (b) Bxe4

(a) Black has every reason to expect victory but allowed too much counterplay by 1...c4?; 2.Rxf5! gxf5; 3.Ng3 and suddenly my kingside was a shambles. The best defense now is 3...Qf6 but Black has already dissipated his advantage and the game was later drawn.

(b) Today I wouldn't hesitate to part with the two bishops by 1...Bxe4; 2.dxe4 c4; 3.Bf4 b5. White's bishop on a2 will remain an overgrown pawn and Black's material advantage should prevail without too much trouble.

Chapter 3

MISJUDGING THREATS

"The threat is stronger than its execution." — Chess Adage

Sometimes players forget that it's necessary to avoid losing before they can win or draw. This may sound obvious, but many games are lost because we get obsessed with our own schemes and forget what the other guy is doing.

Each time your opponent makes a move, stop everything and ask yourself, "What's he threatening?"

HALT!

Cultivate defensive driving. Look at the entire board. If his move contains a threat, how serious is it? If not, why did he make it?

Once you assess the position it's time to decide on your reply. Now ask yourself which move you would like to play in an ideal world. Usually there's a good reason why this dream move isn't playable, but occasionally you'll surprise yourself and create a genuine brilliancy.

LOOK AHEAD

You have to consider the follow-up before deciding on your move. Here White is faced with a hard decision: whether to save his pawn on c4 by pushing it or protecting it.

HOROWITZ - EVANS
USA Championship, 1971

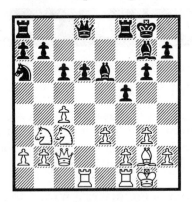

42. White moves
(a) Ne2 (b) c5

(a) White unwisely decided to defend the pawn by 1.Ne2 and was catapulted by force into a lost ending after 1...Nb4; 2.Qd2 Bxc4; 3.Qxb4 Bxe2; 4.Rxd6 Qb6; 5.Qxb6 axb6; 6.Re1 Bc4; 7.Rc1 Bf7; 8.Rd7 Rxa2; 9.Nd4 Rb8; 10.b4 Be8; 11.Bf1 b5; 12.Rc7 Be5; 13.Re7 Bf6; 14.Re6 Kf7 and White resigns. I had expected 15.Bxb5! Bxd4! (not 15...cxb5?; 16 Rc7+) 16.Bc4 Ra1!; 17.Rxa1 Bxa1 rendering the discovered check meaningless because White can't regain the piece.

(b) What a difference a move makes! With a little more thought White could have solved his tiny problem by 1.c5 d5 and only now 2.Ne2 with a long struggle in the offing.

A THREAT IGNORED

The famous artist Marcel Duchamp blithely ignored my threat to win a pawn. It cost him the game.

DUCHAMP - EVANS
New York State Championship, 1948

43. White moves
(a) Qf1 (b) Nc3

(a) The game looks level except for my single threat to snag a pawn by Ngxf2. For better or worse White has no choice other than the passive retreat 1.Qf1 (stronger than 1.Qe1 Qd3; 2.Re2 Rc8). I considered 1...Rd8 (1...Ng5 can be thwarted by 2.Nbd2) 2.h3 Qd1; 3.Rc1 Ngxf2!; 4.Rxd1 Rxd1; 5.Ne1 Rxb1; 6.Kh2! (a pretty trap is 6.Qe2? Nd3!; 7.Qxd3 Rxe1+; 8.Kh2 Rh1+!; 9.Kxh1 Nf2+; 10.Kg1 Nxd3) 6...f5; 7.Qe2 Rd1. White is all tied up but it's not clear that Black can win this ending.

(b) Instead White ignored the threat and made it easy by 1.Nc3? Ngxf2; 2.Nxe4 Nxe4; 3.Nd4 h6 winning a pawn. Duchamp lost 30 moves later.

TOO MANY CHOICES

White's only threat is Qxc7. It can be met in a number of ways — but not by the obvious one.

EVANS - SMITH
USA Open, 1951

44. Black moves
(a) Rdc8 (b) Rcc8

(a) Black thought he was breaking a pin with 1...Rdc8? but overlooked that it costs the exchange after 2.Ba6! Bb7; 3.Rxc7 and he resigned without further ado.

(b) Black's position is fundamentally sound and he has many good moves. Adequate is 1...Rcc8 and if 2.Ba6 Rd5; 3.Qe2 Rcd8. Also sufficient is 1...Qe7 or Nd5.

CREATING YOUR OWN MESS
Danger lurks even in positions without any direct threats. Here neither side has an advantage and I was wondering how to avoid a draw until my opponent created his own mess.

WATERMAN - EVANS
Lone Pine, 1971

45. White moves
(a) Kg2 (b) Bf4

(a) It's hard to see how anyone can make progress after 1.Kg2.

(b) Black was given a chance to invade on the weak dark squares after 1.Bf4? Bxf4; 2.Qxf4 Qf6; 3.Qf2 Qxf2+; 4.Kxf2 Kf6; 5.Kg3 h6; 6.a3 g5; 7.Bc6 Ke5; 8.Kf2 d5; 9.cxd5 Bxd5; 10.Be8 Bb3; 11.Kf3 Bd1+; 12.Kg3 Ba4; 13.Kf3 a6; 14.Kg3 Bxb5; 15.Bxb5 axb5; 16.h4 gxh4+; 17.Kxh4 Kf4; 18.Kh5 Kg3. White resigns.

CHALLENGING THE CENTER

An exciting game can be anticipated when both players castle on opposite wings. Often the struggle for the initiative then takes places in the center before action begins on either flank.

EVANS - WEINBERGER
USA Championship, 1968

46. Black moves
(a) c5 (b) Nc6

(a) Black wants to play 1...e5 but sees that it costs a pawn after 2.dxe5 because of the pin along the d-file. Yet he overlooked a similar but less obvious pin by 1...c5?; 2.dxc5 bxc5; 3.Bxc5. A pawn down, he lost the ending after 3...Qa5; 4.Ba3 Nc6; 5.Nd5.

(b) A normal game with chances for both sides would ensue after 1...Nc6; 2.h4 e5 challenging the center without any material loss.

OVERBURDENED QUEEN

White is bearing down on the long diagonal against g7. This square is amply protected by the queen, isn't it?

EVANS - BISGUIER
USA Championship, 1973

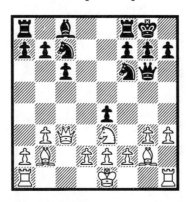

47. Black moves
(a) Re8 (b) Nfd5

(a) After 1...Re8 overprotecting the pawn on e4, it's doubtful whether White retains much of an advantage despite the two bishops or sustained pressure along the a1-h8 diagonal.

(b) Trying to squech an imaginary threat on the long diagonal, Bisguier made the mistake of unmasking it by 1...Nfd5? This error cost a key central pawn after 2.Nxd5 Nxd5; 3.Bxe4! f5 (of course not 3...Qxe4?; 4.Qxg7 mate; or 3...Nxc3; 4.Bxg6 Nxe2; 5.Bd3) 4.Bxd5+ cxd5; 5.h4 h5; 6.Qd4 and Black succumbed shortly.

TRANSPOSING MOVES
Despite an extra pawn I had good reason to be nervous. Black has threats to my back rank combined with a dangerous passed pawn.

EVANS - SANTASIERE
New York, 1947

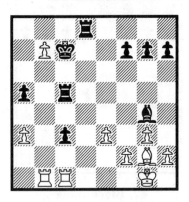

48. White moves
(a) Rb3 (b) h3

(a) I played 1.Rb3? expecting 1...c2; 2.Be4! Rd1+; 3 Kg2 and wins. However, I overlooked 1...Kb8!; 2.h3 (if 2.Rxc3? Rxc3; 3.Rxc3 Rd1+; 4.Bf1 Bh3 forces mate; the only chance now is 2.Be4 f5; 3.Bc2) 2...c2!; 3.hxg4 Rd1+; 4.Kh2 Rxc1; 5.Rd3 Rd1 and White resigns.

(b) Transposing moves gains a precious tempo. 1 h3! serves the dual function of making "luft" for the king while forcing the bishop to retreat. A plausible continuation might be 1...Bf5 (now 1...c2? doesn't work against 2.b8/Q+! Rxb8; 3.Rxb8 Kxb8; 4.hxg4) 2.e4 Bd7 (if 2...Be6 3 Rc2 neutralizes the c-pawn) 3.Rb3 c2; 4.Rd3! and if 4...Kxb7; 5 Rd2! snagging the c-pawn.

THE IMPOSSIBLE DREAM
Before making a move, ask yourself which move you would like to make if you could. Usually you will discover how this dream move is refuted, but a deeper look might reveal why it's possible.

EVANS - MACCIONI
Dubrovnik Olympiad, 1950

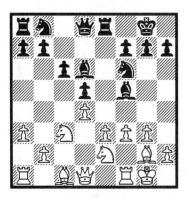

49. White moves
(a) g4 (b) e4

(a) I first reached this position arising from the Nimzo-Indian Defense in Evans - Horne, Hastings 1949. Of course I yearned for 1.e4 but it didn't seem possible because this square is covered by Black four times and only three times by White. So play continued 1.g4? Be6; 2.h3 c5 and suddenly e4 has completely lost its sting.

(b) A year later I found a way to gain two pieces for a rook by carrying out the impossible dream: 1.e4! fxe4; 2.fxe4 Bxe4; 3.Rxf6! (a neat tactical trick) 3...Bxg2; 4.Rxd6! (a crushing zwischenzug) 4...Qxd6; 5.Kxg2 Nd7; 6.Bf4 Qg6; 7.Qb1 Qh5; 8.Qd3 Nb6; 9.Rf1. It took many more moves to exploit White's advantage, but the rest was essentially a pleasant matter of technique.

A DRAFTY KINGSIDE

Attacks against the king are inherently dangerous because they can cause instant capitulation no matter what else is happening or how much material you have in your pocket. Here I was two pawns up but had to exercise care because I was short of time and my kingside was drafty.

EVANS - GREFE
Lone Pine, 1973

50. White moves
(a) Be7 (b) Qf2

(a) Punishment was swift for neglecting the back rank weakness after 1.Be7?? Nh3!; 2.Qe2 Qd2! and I resigned.

(b) It's hard to see how Black can hold out much longer after 1.Qf2! Kh7 (of no avail is 1...Nh3; 2.Qxf7+ Kh7; 3.Ne1) 2.Ne1! Nxd3; 3.Qxf7 Nxe1; 4.Qf2 Nd3; 5.Qg3.

A TIMELY OFFER

I was overall high scorer (90%) in the first postwar Olympiad held in Yugoslavia. While stretching my legs between moves I witnessed an extraordinary double error in this position where White's king seemed perfectly safe. Then Reshevsky, playing first board on the American team, made a horrible move that could have cost us the match against Greece. But he was saved by presence of mind.

RESHEVSKY - MASTICHIADIS
Dubrovnik Olympiad, 1950

51. White moves
(a) Nd2 (b) Bf1

(a) Reshevsky was fixated on the threat of Nxe3. He played 1 Nd2? to stop it (1...Nxe3; 2.Re1) and promptly offered a draw before Black could find the crushing 1...Nxf2! Awed by his reputation, Black accepted with alacrity.

Moral: All's fair in love and chess. Be awfully suspicious when a higher rated opponent offers you a draw out of the blue.

(b) After 1.Bf1 White doesn't have to worry about threats to his king and can proceed with his queenside offensive. If 1...Nxe3?; 2.Re1 snares the pinned knight. Also bad is 1...Nxf2?; 2 Qxf2.

WALKING INTO A FORK

A fork is a double attack, usually by a knight. Many beginners have trouble mastering the tricky gyrations of the only piece that can leap over friendly or enemy units.

GLOVER - EVANS
USA Open, 1948

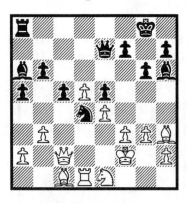

52. White moves
(a) Qc3 (b) Qb2

(a) White's queen is attacked. He made the mistake of moving it into a fork by 1.Qc3? Ne2!; 2.Qc2 Nxc1; 3.Rxc1 Bxc1; 4.Qxc1 c4; 5.bxc4 Qc5+ and Black's material advantage soon proved decisive.

(b) After 1.Qb2 Bxc1; 2.Rxc1 Black's pieces are a little more active but he has no crusher in sight. Also playable is 1.Rxd4 Bxc1; 2.Rd1.

HELP FROM OUR FRIENDS

White has a slight space advantage but it's hard to see how to make progress against staunch defense. But wait — Black's on move — maybe he'll overlook my only threat and find a way to go wrong!

EVANS - JIMENEZ
Havana, 1964

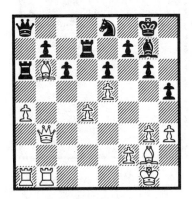

53. Black moves
(a) Nc7 (b) Qc8

(a) Black simply lost the exchange by 1...Nc7? overlooking 2.Bf1! Nd5; 3.Bxa6 Qxa6; 4.Bc5 and the rest was a matter of technique.

(b) A draw is likely after the solid 1...Qc8; 2.Bf1 Ra8. Perhaps Black overlooked Bf1 because he didn't expect it to abandon its strong post along the h1-a8 diagonal — ye old switcheroo.

THE GUARD THAT FAILED

White must find a way to guard against the single threat of Bxb2 winning a pawn. This simple task is harder than it looks.

JACKSON - EVANS
Canadian Open, 1966

54. White moves
(a) Nd4 (b) b3

(a) White rejected 1.Qc2 Rfc8; 2.Nbd2 b3!; 3.Nxb3 Nxa4. Instead he decided to defend the pawn with 1.Nd4? Bxd4!; 2.exd4 (not 2.Qxd4? Nb3) 2...Nxa4!; 3.b3 (if 3.Qxa4 Qxe2) 3...Nb6 and Black's extra pawn proved decisive.

(b) Necessary is 1.b3 Rfc8; 2.Bb5 with even chances.

ONE-TWO PUNCH

White will regain the pawn and get the better game. Meanwhile Black, facing mate-in-one, learns that it does no good to defend against one threat and overlook another.

EVANS - KRAMER
USA Open, 1949

55. Black moves
(a) Qf7 (b) g6

(a) After 1...Qf7?; 2.Rc8+ Rxc8; 3.Qxc8+ Qf8; 4.Qe6+ Black resigned since he must lose a bishop.

(b) The only defense is 1...g6 and if 2.Qxf4 Rf8 offers fair chances to hold the game.

CARELESS DEFENSE

Black is cramped but solid. White has an obvious advantage in space but can't make any immediate inroads.

EVANS - KESTEN
Dubrovnik Olympiad, 1950

56. Black moves
(a) Bb7 (b) Kh8

(a) The natural developing move 1...Bb7? gave White a way to invade with 2.e4 Nf4; 3.Nf5! Qc7; 4.e5 fxe5; 5.dxe5 Nd5; 6.Nd6 Re7; 7.Nd4 a6; 8.Bb3 c5; 9.Nxe6 Nxe6;10.Nxb7 snaring a pawn.

(b) Black can avoid a ton of trouble by playing 1...Kh8 before Bb7 when a long struggle lies ahead.

DESPERATE MEASURES

When you know you are losing, make things as messy as possible. Here Black just offered a knight (Nf5e3) to gum up the works against the FIDE world champion. Should he accept the sacrifice – or ignore it?

KARPOV - ANAND
Dos Hermanas, 1997

57. White moves
(a) fxe3 (b) Nce5

(a) Black's compensation for the knight is illusory after 1.fxe3! Qg6; 2.Rad1. However, Karpov's temperament worked against him — he prefers clear, simple solutions instead of messy complications, especially with the merciless ticking of the clock.

(b) Despite a big advantage, White only drew after 1.Nce5?! Nc2; 2.Nc6?! (Karpov notes that he missed "an easy win" with 2.a5! Nxe1; 3.Rxe1 Bxa5; 4.Qxa5 Qxb5; 5.Qxa7 netting another pawn) 2...Nxa1; 3.Rxa1 Ra8; 4.Re1 e5; 5.Rxe5 Qf7; 6.a5 Qb3; 7.Ncb4 Rae8; 8.Rxe8 Rxe8; 9.Kh2 Qf7; 10.axb6 Qh5+; 11.Kg1 Qd1+; with perpetual check.

Anand explained that his predicament was already desperate: "I felt quite calm here. Once you understand you are lost, you can do anything you want. At the time I thought 1.Nce5 was best. After the game, I thought it was second-best and now I'm not so sure. When somebody is looking to collect a piece and come out smelling like a rose, you want to make him work as hard as possible and calculate hard. Often this is your best chance of getting counterplay. The advantage of my knight sacrifice is that it creates a lot of complications. This is the best way to fight, to make the game as messy as possible.

"If you go in for simple lines most players, and especially Karpov, will calculate everything straight through. In such positions your opponent wants the game to be over quickly. He wants to avoid complications. He wants concrete lines. So you make a lot of threats. Afterwards it's very easy to see everything clearly, but during the game you have to make one move at a time, to be very concrete, and it's not easy.

"I thought 1.fxe3 would have won. It looks like I have to play 1...Qg6 because if 1...fxe3 he simply takes 2.Nxb6 axb6; 3.Rxe3 and I have no way of trapping his Queen. After the game I asked Karpov if he wanted to analyze and he said: 'There is nothing to analyze. White was completely winning.' "

SWEET SIMPLICITY

Black lacks a direct threat but is clearly better because of White's curious pawn structure (with weaknesses on c2 and g4). Instead of waiting for the roof to cave in, White should try to ease the pressure right now with timely exchanges.

STEINER - EVANS
8th match game, 1952

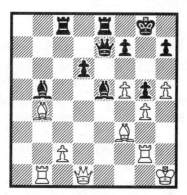

58. White moves
(a) Ba5 (b) Bxd6

(a) The dilatory 1.Ba5? led to trouble after 1...Bc6; 2.Bb4 Qb7; 3.Bxc6 Qxc6; 4.Bd2 h6; 5.Be3 Re7; 6.Bd4 Bxd4; 7.Qxd4 Re2; 8.Rag1 Qf3; 9.Qxd6 Rcxc2; 10.Qd8+ Kh7. White resigns.

(b) White should take this opportunity to simplify by 1.Bxd6! Qxd6; 2.Qxd6 Bxd6; 3.Rxb5 Re1+; 4.Rg1 Rxg1+; 5.Kxg1 Rxc2; 6.Rb7 when the opposite colored bishops should assure a draw.

ANY MOVE DOESN'T WIN!

Overconfidence can be a big enemy. Here I was two pawns ahead and didn't see any danger on the horizon despite a slight threat to capture my queen.

EVANS - STEINER
9th match game, 1952

59. White moves
(a) Qc6 (b) Qc7

(a) Thinking any queen move would win, I played 1.Qc6? expecting 1...Bxf1; 2.Rxf1 with no further problems. To my consternation, however, I had to settle for a draw after 1...Be4!; 2.fxe4 Ng4; 3.Rfe1 Qxh2+; 4.Kf1 Ne5!; 5.Qc2 Qh1+; 6.Ke2 Qf3+ with perpetual check.

(b) White can anticipate victory with 1.Qc7! Bxf1 (not 1...Ng4?; 2.fxg4 Be4; 3.f3; no better is 1...Be4; 2.Qxe7 Re8; 3.Qxe8+ Nxe8; 4.fxe4) 2.Rxf1 Nd5; 3.Qc2 and the extra material should prevail in the long run.

ANTICIPATING THE INEVITABLE

Max Euwe was the most error-prone world champion. He lost his title in the 1937 rematch to Alexander Alekhine largely because he failed to cope with all the tactical nuances that were thrown at him. Here White is threatening Kg2 and Nf3 trapping the queen. Watch what happened!

ALEKHINE - EUWE
10th match game, 1937

60. Black moves
(a) Nc6 (b) h6

(a) After 1...Nc6?; 2.Kg2 Nxe5; 3.dxe5 Nh5; 4.gxh5 Black resigned in a few more moves. No better is 1...Qxh3; 2.Rd3 Qh4; 3.Kg2 trapping the queen with Rh3 or Rh1.

(b) Simply 1...h6; 2.Kg2 Nh7 creates an escape route for the knight and queen. On 3.d5 exd5; 4.cxd5 Nc4! is better than 4...f6?; 5.Nf3 Rxe2; 6.Rxe2!

EXCESSIVE CAUTION

Karpov had already won the first game in this FIDE title match. He could have increased his lead to two points but timidity and excessive caution cost him this game even though he managed to defend his crown in a speedy playoff after a 3-3 tie.

ANAND - KARPOV
2nd match game, 1998

61. Black moves
(a) h6 (b) Ne2+

(a) Black made "luft" by 1...h6? to defend against the threat of Qf7 and Qf8 mate (hoping for 2.Rxc2? Ne2+; 3.Rxe2 Qc1) but fell afoul of 2.Qf7+ Kh8; 3.Re3! with the double threat of Rxc2 or Rxe5. Suddenly a won game turned into a lost one after 3...d4 (if 3...Ne4; 4.Re2 followed by Rxc2) 4.Rxe5 d3; 5.Bd4 Rg8; 6.Re6 d2; 7.Rxc6 dxc1=Q+; 8.Kh2 Qd2 9.Rc8 and Black resigns.

(b) The simplest path to victory is 1...Ne2+!; 2.Kf1 Qe8!; 3.Kxe2 Bb8+; 4.Re3 Qb5+ followed by Bxa7. Black became too worried about protecting his own king yet failed to realize the opposing king was even more unsafe.

SACRIFICIAL SHOCK

Dr. Tarrasch noted that an unexpected sacrifice often gives rise to an element of shock that hinders calm and clear thinking. His theory explains many blunders committed under the influence of what the good doctor diagnosed as "sacrificial shock."

ROMI - STALDI
Italian Championship, 1954

62. Black moves
(a) Kf8 (b) Kxh7

(a) White jettisoned his queen to check on h7. Of course 1...Kf8?; 2.Qh8 mates. The strangest part of this story is that Black never made another move! Thinking his game would be hopeless once White created a new queen with discovered check, he resigned on the spot. Obviously gremlins were at work.

(b) The correct defense is 1...Kxh7; 2.f8/Q+ Kg6; 3.Rg7+ (if 3.Qxc8 Rf1+; 4.Kh2 Qf4+; 5.g3 Qf2 mate) 3...Kh6! and Black emerges a rook ahead no matter how you slice it.

NIL DESPERANDUM

Never despair! A defeatist attitude clouds judgment and prevents you from offering the toughest resistance in an inferior position. If you believe you're going to lose, you'll lose!

TAL - MATANOVIC
Bled, 1961

63. Black moves
(a) Nf6   (b) Rg4

(a) Black's position is ugly yet not totally bereft of hope. After 1...Nf6?; 2.Bxe4 Nxe4+; 3.Ke1 Nf6; 4.Qh8 the two minor pieces were no match for the omnipotent queen.

(b) The correct defense is 1...Rg4!; 2.Bxf5 (if 2.Qh8 Rg2+; 3.Be2 Nf6 with the double threat of Rg8 or Bg4) 2...Rxg7; 3.hxg7 Nf6; 4.Bh7. Black probably analyzed this far and concluded that further resistance was futile but now 4...Ng8!; 5.Bxg8 Kf6; 6.Bh7 Kxg7; 7.Bf5 b6 offers good drawing chances.

Chapter 4

IGNORING PINS

"The pin is mightier than the sword." — Fred Reinfeld

The pin is by far the most frequently encountered tactical theme. A pinned piece is immobilized because it must shield a more valuable piece (or square) behind it.

There are two kinds of pins: absolute and relative. An absolute pin means the pinned piece can't move because doing so exposes the king to capture, which is illegal. A relative pin means the piece is free to move, but at its own peril.

In general it's a good idea to break pins as soon as possible. But they aren't always so easy to spot, as shown in the next example.

HIDDEN PINS

It's usually easy to recognize a pin: a piece of lesser value can't move without dropping something that's worth more behind it. Here a relatively harmless, obscure pin seems to present no immediate danger. But, as usual, neglect proves fatal.

POLUGAEVSKY-HORT
Manila, 1975

64. White moves
(a) Qd7 (b) g3

(a) 1 Rd7 is the only place White can move his rook without costing material, but White is in no hurry to swap queens. Instead he broke the pin by the natural 1.Qd7? and probably expected 1...Rf8. But 1...Re1+!; 2.Kh2 Rc1 suddenly set up a new pin — this time against the king instead of the queen. White resigned.

(b) The most sensible move is 1.g3 making "luft" for the king on g2. White thus retains the initiative and averts disaster.

DELAYED PINS

Some pins rear their ugly head a move or two later. In this position, can you pinpoint where the danger is likely to occur?

KASHDAN-EVANS
Hollywood, 1954

65. White moves
(a) cxb5 (b) b3

(a) White can avoid losing a pawn 1.cxb5 c4! (better than 1...axb5; 2.b4!) 2.Qe2 axb5.

(b) Instead White tried to bolster his center by 1.b3? and walked into a pin after 1...b4; 2.Ne2 Nxe4!; 3.Qxe4 Bf5; 4.Qh4 Bxb1; 5.Bg5 Bxa2; 6.Bxe7 Qd7; 7.Ng5 h6; 8.Ne4 f5. His attack doesn't compensate for his material loss but I later refused a draw and lost on time, a painful lesson that cost me first prize.

HALLUCINATIONS

One reason for dragging out wretched positions to the bitter end is that you never know if or when your opponent will go wrong along the way. A case in point.

ROMANOVSKY - KASPARIAN
Leningrad, 1938

66. Black moves
(a) Rxh3+ (b) Qb4

(a) Kasparian, a noted problem composer, forgot that his knight was pinned and announced mate with 1...Rxh3+?; 2.Bxh3 (not 2.Kxh3 Qh4 mate) 2...Nf3. This move was actually made on the board until his opponent, somewhat embarrassed, reminded him that moving a pinned piece is illegal. "At first he failed to understand me and it was only after I gesticulated along the a1-h8 diagonal that he saw his mistake and returned the knight to e5," wrote Romanovsky.

Black resigned after giving away his rook. This hallucination came about because his attention was riveted on a small sector of the board. At that instant all else ceased to exist.

(b) Black's extra pawn must prevail after 1...Qb4. His position is so overwhelming that even a quiet waiting move like 1...Qe3 is sufficient for victory.

DOUBLE HALLUCINATION

A draw is likely in the endgame when material is level. Black's bishop is pinned and his rook is attacked, yet he still retains an edge because the bishop is stronger than the knight.

EBRALIDZE - RAGOZIN
USSR Championship, 1937

67. Black moves
(a) Rc7 (b) Rc3

(a) Incredibly, Ragozin quickly played 1...Rc7?? thinking that 2.Rxc7 Bd6+ regains the rook. But the bishop can't move because it's pinned. A spectator, unable to restrain himself, shouted, "Archil, take the rook!" Ebralidze replied, "I can see — don't interfere!" After a few minutes White retreated 2.Rd5? causing a commotion in the playing hall. At first Ebralidze, then a young expert, didn't understand what it was all about. He looked up in surprise before realizing his error and clutched his head in despair. Blindly believing in the authority of his famous opponent, the comedy of errors continued with 2...Bf6; 3.Nb5 Rc2+; 4.Kg3 a6; 5.Rd7+ Ke8; 6.Rc7 Be5+ and White resigned.

(b) On 1...Rc3; 2.Rxa7 Kf6 the bishop can efficiently support the advance of the kingside pawns, but a draw is still likely after 3.Kg2.

PIN CUSHIONS

My opponent refused a draw a few moves ago. Perhaps the need to justify that decision explains his persistence in playing for a win even though the tide was now turning in my favor.

COMMONS - EVANS
USA Championship, 1974

68. White moves
(a) Bxa6 (b) Rf2

(a) White should settle for a draw by 1.Bxa6 Rxb2; 2.Re2. He didn't avail himself of this opportunity because he was still chasing the chimera of the advantage he once had.

(b) White failed to perceive the danger and allowed himself to become a pin cushion by defending his second rank while overlooking a serious threat to his third rank. After 1.Rf2? Rb3!; 2.Rd2 Bb5; 3.Ra1 Kf7 it became apparent that there was no easy way to break the pin since 4.Ke2 Bxd3+; 5.Rxd3 Rxb2+ snares a pawn. The best chance is 4.Ra3 Rxa3; 5.bxa3 Rc3; 6.Ke2 Rxa3; 7.Bxb5 axb5; 8.Rb2 with a probable draw. However, as usually happens, one mistake leads to another and it concluded quickly after 4.h4?! h5; 5.g4? (still 5.Ke2 is necessary) 5...hxg4; 6.Rg1 Bxd3; 7.Rxd3 Rxb2; 8.Rxg4 Rcc2; 9.Ra3 Rh2; 10.Kf3 Rxh3+; 11.Rg3 Rxh4; 12.Rxa6 Rb4; 13.f5 gxf5; 14.Ra7+ Kf6. White resigns.

THE PIN THAT FAILED

Black has enough extra material to win as he pleases. White was ready to resign but had one last trick up his sleeve.

PAVEY - HOROWITZ
USA Championship, 1951

69. Black moves
(a) Kb6 (b) Qxf3+

(a) The pin by 1...Ra3? can be met by 2.Qe7+. But it's hard to see how White can live much longer after 1...Kb6.

(b) Instead Black saw an "easy" win by pin with 1...Qxf3+?; 2.Qxf3 Ra3. But he was startled by 3.Kh4!! Rxf3 stalemate!

BREAKING A PIN

A bishop hammering a knight is the most common pin. Usually there is a right way and a wrong way to prevent any damage by breaking the pin before it becomes too menacing.

NEUSTADTER - EVANS
Los Angeles, 1973

70. White moves
(a) Bxd4 (b) h3

(a) The right way to rid himself of the pesky pin is 1.Bxd4 exd4; 2.Ne2 c5; 3.h3 putting the question to the bishop – either swap or retreat. Black would retain an edge thanks to his two bishops, but this is far better than what happened in the game.

(b) The wrong way is 1.h3? Nxf3+; 2.Bxf3 Bxh3 costing a pawn. The game ended quickly after 3.Bg2 Qd7; 4.d4 Bxg2; 5.Kxg2 f5; 6.dxe5 Bxe5; 7.f4 Bxc3; 8.bxc3 Qc6 and White resigns.

CREATING COUNTERTHREATS

Sometimes the only way to break a pin is by allowing it to be carried out! To do so, however, you have to create an even greater threat against some enemy weak point.

POPIEL - MARCO
Monte Carlo, 1902

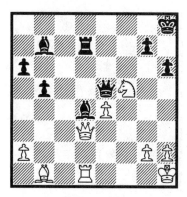

71. Black moves
(a) g6 (b) Bg1

(a) On 1...g6?, 2.Nxd4 simply wins a piece by executing the initial threat to capture the pinned bishop.

(b) So powerful is the spell exerted by a pin that Black resigned on the spot because his bishop on d4 looks doomed. He failed to see that 1...Bg1! threatening Qxh2 mate turns the tables. White has nothing better than 2.Kxg1 Rxd3; 3.Bxd3 Bxe4; 4.Bxe4 Qxe4 and the queen is boss. This example of premature resignation was cited in enough books to assure Popiel of negative immortality.

Moral: You can't win by resigning.

A WICKED PIN

White is understandly reluctant to recapture the knight on c6 right away. Instead he tries to increase the pressure, but is it wise to wait?

KORCHNOI - FISCHER
Curacao, 1962

72. White moves
(a) Rc1 (b) dxc6

(a) Korchnoi played 1 Rc1? on the assumption that 1...Nxb4 is refuted by 2.Qb2+ followed by Rxc7. But Fischer crossed him up by 1...Qa7!; 2.Qb2+ Nce5 blocking the check and keeping the extra piece. White resigned.

(b) White should recapture without further ado. After 1.dxc6 Qxc6 a draw is the likely outcome.

A ROYAL PAIN

Pins inflict pain, especially when a queen and king are lined up on an open file. This lesson was brought home in one of my first tournament games at the Marshall Club Junior Championship.

GOMPERT - EVANS
New York, 1946

73. White moves
(a) c3 (b) Ng5

(a) White should bolster his extra pawn by 1.c3 0-0-0; 2.Bd2 Rhe8; 3.0-0-0 but probably was worried about 3...Qe6. However, this can be met by 4.Ng5 (of course not 4.b3?? Ba3 mate; nor 4.Qc4 Bd5; 5.Qa4 Bxa2) 4...Qxa2; 5.Nxe4 Qa1+; 6.Kc2 Qa4+; 7.Kb1 Rxe4; 8.Qf3 Rde8; 9.Bd3 with a beautiful game.

(b) White was in a hurry to simplify and neglected development by moving the same piece twice but overlooked the loss of a pawn with 1.Ng5? Bxc2!; 2.Qxe7+ Bxe7; 3.Nf3 0-0-0. Suddenly Black has the better endgame thanks to pressure against the isolani on d4.

ABSENT-MINDED GRANDMASTER

The great Akiba Rubinstein fell into the same trap twice in a
span of two years. He wasn't the only paladin to succumb to
this sort of pitfall (see diagram 41).

ALEKHINE - RUBINSTEIN
San Remo, 1930

74. Black moves
(a) f5 (b) Nef6

(a) The only problem with 1...f5? is 2.Nxd5! and the knight is
immune due to a hidden pin (2...cxd5?; 3.Bc7 traps the queen).
Anyone can overlook this trick, but Rubinstein fell for it just
two years earlier against Euwe at Bad Kissingen in 1928!

(b) It's still a hard game after the necessary retreat 1...Nef6.

SHUN DOUBLED PAWNS

Black has already freed his game and wrested the initiative. White's immediate problem is how to meet the threat of Nxd3+.

GOLDWATER - EVANS
New York, 1948

75. White moves
(a) Bc2 (b) Be2

(a) White walked into a pin that ruined his pawn structure after 1.Bc2? Bg4!; 2.h3 Bxf3; 3.Nxf3 Nxf3+; 4.Qxf3 Qxf3; 5.gxf3 Bc5; 6.Rg1 g6; 7.Rg5 0-0-0; 8.Be3 Rhe8 giving Black a marked endgame advantage.

(b) White should try to steer for equality with 1.Be2.

MY IMMORTAL ZUGZWANG GAME

Zugzwang is a German word meaning the unpleasant obligation to move. Here Black is severely cramped, yet he might be able to hold with precise defense since there are no obvious points of entry.

EVANS - POPEL
Canadian Open, 1966

76. Black moves
(a) Nf8 (b) Qd8

(a) Black voluntarily submitted to an ugly pin by 1...Nf8? and now had to lose a pawn to zugzwang after 2.Qa8! Rf7 (Black would like to pass but can't!) 3.Bxg6 Rxf3; 4.Kxf3 Kg7; 5.Bf5 e4+; 6.Bxe4 Nd7; 7.Qa1+ Ne5+; 8.Kg3 Qd7; 9.Qd1 Nxc4; 10.Qh5 Kg8; 11.Qg6+ Kf8; 12.Qf6+ Qf7; 13.Qxf7+ Kxf7; 14 h5 and Black resigns.

(b) Black must first safeguard his back rank by retreating with 1...Qd8! White retains a bind but a forced win is problematical.

ONE PIN DESERVES ANOTHER

Black threatens to invade with his rook by 1...Rc2+ (2.Qxc2? d3+). White's predicament is precarious but not hopeless.

PILNICK - EVANS
Santa Monica, 1964

77. White moves
(a) Rd2 (b) Qxd4

(a) White protected his second rank by 1.Rd2? which in turn left his back rank vulnerable after 1...Rc1; 2.Rd1 Bf5; 3.Qd2 d3+; 4.Qe3 Rxf1+; 5.Kxf1 Qxe3. Another mistake would be 1.Kg1? Rc3; 2.Qxd4 Qxd4+; 3.Rxd4 Rc1 pinning the knight.

(b) White feared walking into a pin by 1.Qxd4! Rc2+; 2.Ke1 Qxd4; 3.Rxd4 Rc1+; 4.Rd1 Rxd1+; 5.Kxd1 Bxf1 but the saving resource now is 1.Qxd4! Rc2+; 2.Ke3! taking the king for a stroll. It looks dangerous but there is no other way to avoid losing a piece. 2...Qe6+; 3.Qe4 Rxa2; 4.Qxe6 Bxe6; 5.Nd2 offers good drawing chances. It's certainly better than what happened in the game!

PILING ON

The beauty of a pin is that it doesn't just run away. Often you can pile on more and more pressure until it becomes unbearable.

EVANS - PORTISCH
Amsterdam, 1971

78. Black moves
(a) Rd8 (b) Ne4

(a) White's in big trouble after 1...Rd8! because if 2.Kh2 getting out of the potential pin then 2...Rcd6 threatens Rxd4. Now 3.Rfe3 Qd7 wins material by piling on more pressure against the doomed bishop at d4.

(b) Instead Black let me off the hook by 1...Ne4?; 2 Be3! and a draw was agreed since if 2...Ng5; 3.Bxg5 hxg5; 4.Kh2 safely gets out of the pin along the h1-a8 diagonal.

ADVANCE OR RETREAT?

White's queen is attacked. He has a choice between moving it out of harm's way or interposing a piece.

JACKSON - GOLOMBEK
London, 1932

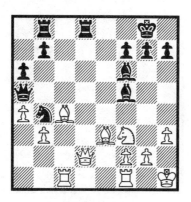

79. White moves
(a) Nd4 (b) Qe1

(a) White imprudently stepped into a pin with 1.Nd4? Rd7; 2.g4 Bg6 (stronger is Rbd8!) 3.Nc6! saving the pinned piece. But Black could have netted two pieces for a rook by 1...Rxd4!; 2.Bxd4 Rd8 setting up a devastating pin along the d-file. Instead the game ultimately was drawn.

(b) White rejected 1.Qe2? b5! trapping the bishop. The correct retreat is 1.Qe1 (hoping to exploit a pin of his own with Bd2) and if 1...b5; 2.axb5 axb5; 3.Be2 averts material loss.

PINS GAIN TIME

Black is an exchange down and faces a dilemma. Swapping queens will lead to a lost ending but avoiding it will cost a bishop.

ROHACEK - MAY
Bad Sliac, 1932

80. Black moves
(a) Qxe1+   (b) Rc1

(a) Black lost after 1...Qxe1+?; 2.Rxe1 Bxh3; 3.Rb3 Rxb3; 4.axb3 followed by Ra1.

(b) The solution is 1...Rc1! which pins the queen and gains time for a discovered check after 2.Qxc1 Bf3+; 3.Kf1 Bxe2+; 4.Kxe2 Qxe5+; 5.Kf2 Qxb8 snaring two pawns with a won endgame.

GUARDING EMPTY SQUARES

Usually a pinned piece must stay put because it shields something more valuable. But sometimes this piece can't move because it must continue to guard a vital empty square behind it.

BURN - TARRASCH
Breslau, 1889

81. White moves
(a) Rc5 (b) Rfd1

(a) White must find a way to exploit his lead in development before Black gets the bishop out of the box. He tried 1.Rc5? which looks good but lacks an effective follow-up after 1...Qd6. White finally lost many moves later.

(b) If you don't use it, you lose it! White can win by force by bombarding the pinned knight on c6: 1.Rfd1! Qf5 (or 1...Qe6; 2.Bxc6 Nxc6; 3.Qxc6 snares a piece because of the mate on d8) 2.Bxc6 Rxd1+; 3.Rxd1 Nxc6; 4.Rd8+! Nxd8; 5.Qe8 mate (on the vital empty square).

THE WRONG CHECK

Pins take different shapes. An overburdened piece is also vulnerable because it can't defend two places at once.

NIMZOVICH - YATES
Bad Kissingen, 1928

82. Black moves
(a) Qd1+ (b) Qf1+

(a) It doesn't seem to matter which check Black gives — but it does. He played 1...Qd1+?; 2.Kg2 a5? (2...Qg1+? still gets back on the right track) 3.Nxf6+ leading to a draw by perpetual check.

(b) Black missed an easy win by 1...Qf1+; 2.Kg4 Qe2+; 3.Qf3 (or 3.Kxh4 g5+; 4.Kg3 Bf4+) 3...f5+!; 4.Kxf5 Qxf3+. The overburdened king can't protect both f3 and f5.

UNUSUAL DEFENSE

Samuel Reshevsky was famous for getting into horrific time jams. Curiously, it was his opponents, with plenty of time left, who blundered by moving too fast to make him overstep on the clock. After a tense and exhausting struggle this position was reached with four moves left to the time control.

RESHEVSKY - BOLESLAVAKY
Zurich, 1953

83. Black moves
(a) Bc5   (b) Ra7

(a) Sammy won after 1...Bc5?; 2.Rd8+ Bf8; 3.Rdb8 (better than 3.Rbb8 Kg7; 4.Rxf8 b1/Q; 5.Rxb1 Kxf8) picking up the dangerous passed pawn.

(b) Black can save the game by an ingenious pinning maneuver: 1...Ra7!; 2.Rxh7 b1/Q; 3.Rxb1 Kxh7; 4.h4 Bc5; 5.Rb3 Rf7; 6.Rf3 Rxf3; 7.Kxf3 with a draw in view.

Chapter 5

PREMATURE AGGRESSION

"So set up your attacks that when the fire is out, it isn't out!"
Harry Nelson Pillsbury

They have a word for a boxer who goes for an early knockout. He's called a "headhunter." But a fighter who doesn't pace himself often runs out of steam too soon. The same applies to chess.

Reuben Fine wrote: "After only a little experience with the game the average man soon finds that his greatest delights come from a direct attack upon the king. As he becomes more expert he begins to appreciate the subtler nuances of position play, pawn maneuvering, opening strategy, etc. Once again, direct aggression fades more and more. Many critics never get over the naive emphasis on the direct attack and unfortunately fill chess literature with the most ludicrous comments."

Don't make the mistake of launching an offensive with too little, too soon. A successful attack requires patience and firepower. You need to harness your forces to overcome resistance.

SCHOLAR'S MATE

Quick knockouts are enormously appealing to beginners. These ploys usually work a few times until their opponents wise up. Consider 1.e4 e5; 2.Bc4 Bc5; 3.Qh5?! with the horrendous threat of Qxf7 known as Scholar's Mate.

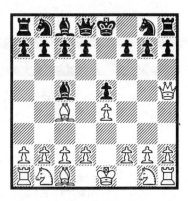

84. Black moves
(a) Nc6 (b) Qe7

(a) White's last move looks dangerous but violates the principle of bringing out the queen too soon. 1...Nc6?? defends the minor threat (to e5) yet overlooks the major one (to f7). It's happened countless times. 2.Qxf7 mate!

(b) White ought to be punished for bringing his queen out so soon, but how? The simplest solution is 1...Qe7 defending both e5 and f7. Now 2.Nf3 Nc6; 3.0-0 Nf6 brings out a new piece with gain of time by taking a potshot at the queen. After 4.Qh4 d6 Black already enjoys a pleasant lead in development.

TILTING AT WINDMILLS

This position arises from the Alekhine-Chatard Attack of the French Defense: 1.e4 e6; 2.d4 d5; 3.Nc3 Nf6; 4.Bg5 Be7; 5.e5 Nfd7; 6.h4!? a6; 7.Qg4 Kf8. White desperately wants to mount an attack at all costs even though Black is rock-solid.

PLATZ - EVANS
USA Championship, 1948

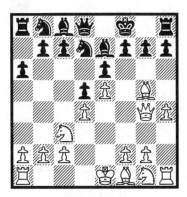

85. White moves
(a) Rh3 (b) Qf4

(a) It's wrong to launch an attack without sufficient force but White went for the jugular by 1.Rh3!? c5; 2.Rf3!? Bxg5!; 3.hxg5 Nc6 undermining White's center. If now 3.Qxe6 Ndxe5 refutes the "attack." Realizing he already had overreached himself, White futilely sacked a rook with 3.Rxf7+ Kxf7; 4.g6+ hxg6; 5.Nf3 Nf8 and Black had nothing more to fear.

(b) Black obviously is preparing ...c5. The right way to shore up the outpost on e5 is 1.Qf4! c5; 2.dxc5 Nc6; 3.Nf3 (the knight belongs here instead of the rook!) 3...Qc7; 4.b4 Ndxe5; 5.Bxe7+ Kxe7; 6.Nxe5 Qxe5+; 7.Qxe5 Nxe5; 8.Na4 with a tough endgame ahead.

SELF-INFLICTED WOUNDS

Launching an offensive without proper preparation is likely to backfire against good defense. The player who is better developed is apt to profit from the open lines.

CASTALDI - TARTAKOWER
Stockholm, 1937

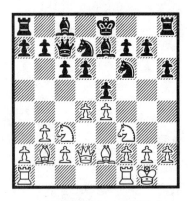

86. Black moves
(a) 0-0 (b) g5

(a) Black has nothing better than 1...0-0 with the hope of slowly working his way out of the cramp.

(b) 1...g5? renders Black's kingside unsafe for habitation. The game was over all too quickly after 2.Rfd1 Nf8; 3.dxe5 dxe5; 4.Nxe5! Be6 (not 4...Qxe5; 5.Nd5 Qxb2; 6.Nc7 mate) 5.Nb5! Qb8 (or 5...cxb5; 6.Bxb5+ N8d7; 7.Nxd7 Bxd7; 8.Bxd7+ Qxd7; 9.Qxd7+ Nxd7; 10.Bxh8) 6.Qa5 Bd8; 7.Rxd8+ Qxd8; 8.Nc7+. Black resigns (8...Ke7; 9 Ba3+).

QUIET MOVES

When actress Mae West was asked for her opinion of a right wing group called the Minute Men, she quipped, "I prefer a man who takes his time." Similarly, when confronted with several ways to pursue an attack, we must decide whether a forcing move or a slower one is more appropriate.

EVANS - LARSEN
San Antonio, 1962

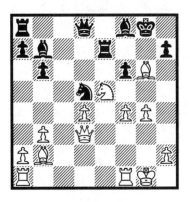

87. White moves
(a) Nf7 (b) Be4

(a) White must lose a piece but has a blistering attack. I chose a forcing continuation which allowed Black to consolidate after 1.Nf7!? Rxf7; 2.Bxf7+ Kxf7; 3.Qxh7+ Bg7; 4.g5 Qd6; 5.g6+ Kf8; 6.Rae1 Nb4; 7.Qh3 Qd5. Eventually the attack ran out of steam and I lost.

(b) After the game Paul Keres suggested the quiet 1.Be4! fxe5; 2.dxe5 Rd7; 3.Qf3! (too fast is 3.e6? Bc5+; 4.Kh1 Nxf4) with three pawns for the piece and a pawn steamroller coming with f5.

BAYONET ATTACK

An attack rarely can succeed while your king is still in the center. But what if you can't decide which way to castle?

STEINER - EVANS
6th match game, 1952

88. White moves
(a) g4 (b) 0-0-0

(a) White launched a bayonet attack with 1.g4!? hoping to get in a rapid h4 and g5. This was foiled by 1...Nc5!; 2.Ne5 (forced; if 2.dxc5 Bxg4 wins the knight on f3 plus several pawns) 2...Nxd3+; 3.Nxd3+ Qh4 and Black gained the upper hand.

(b) If White is bent on attacking at all cost, he should first castle queenside. On 1.0-0-0 Re8 it's anybody's game. 1.0-0 is a safer positional approach.

DODGING THE BULLET

This famous brevity is cited in numerous anthologies. White already sacrificed the exchange and now adds fuel to the fire by offering a bishop at h7.

MARSHALL - BURN
Ostend, 1907

89. Black moves
(a) Kxh7 (b) Kf8

(a) Frank Marshall was renowned for his chess "swindles" and this one worked big-time. Black snatched the bishop and fell afoul of a brilliancy after 1...Kxh7?; 2.Ng5+ Kg6 (no help is 2...Kg8; 3.Qxh5 Nf6; 4.Qxf7+ Kh8; 5.0-0-0 Rf8; 6.Rh1!) 3.Ndf3 e5; 4.Nh4+ Kf6; 5.Nh7+ Ke7; 6.Nf5+ Ke6; 7.Nxg7+ Ke7; 8.Nf5+ Ke6; 9.d5+ Kxf5; 10.Qxh5+ Ke4; 11.0-0-0. Black resigns.

(b) Black can dodge the bullet by 1...Kf8! when White would be hard-put to show compensation for his material deficit. 2.Ng5 Nf6 holds the fort. The anthologies, which feature flashy finishes, are mum about this defense.

BRUTAL OR SUBTLE?

When prosecuting an attack we are often faced with a hard choice between brutal moves or subtle ones. There is no pat formula — each position is as distinct as a fingerprint.

LEVENFISH - SUBAREV
Leningrad, 1925

90. White moves
(a) Rh5+ (b) Rh3

(a) Unable to find a win, White settled for a draw by 1.Rh5+ gxh5; 2.Qxh5+ Kf6; 3.Qh8+ Kg5; 4.Qh5+, etc.

(b) Instead of letting the attack fizzle out with premature checks, the subtle 1.Rh3! (threatening Qh4 mate) mops up after 1...Qxg4+ (or 1...Qxe4+ 2.Bf3) 2.Rg3 c2; 3.h4+ Kf4; 4.Qf6+.

THE QUEEN'S GAMBIT

When learning the names of the openings, I wondered why the queen was sacrificed in so many games. In my naivete, I took "Queen's Gambit" literally before discovering that this so-called gambit involves only the temporary sacrifice of a pawn after 1.d4 d5; 2.Nf3 Nf6; 3.c4 dxc4; 4.Nc3 a6.

SZABO - KERES
Zurich, 1953

91. White moves
(a) e3 (b) Qa4+

(a) The Queen's Gambit is not a "real" gambit because White can always regain the pawn. The simplest method is 1.e3 and if Black tries to hold it with 1...b5 then 2.a4 c6; 3.axb5 cxb5 4.Nxb5 shatters the defensive setup.

(b) Grandmaster Szabo played 1.Qa4+? prompting Bronstein to note in his widely praised tournament book: "Practically speaking, the shortest game of the tournament even though it did continue until the 41st move. After this check Szabo might as well have resigned, since in effect he is now giving Keres odds of pawn and move. One wonders how, after prolonged consideration, Szabo could blunder a pawn as early as move five. Keres was more than a little amazed himself; he spent 15 minutes considering his reply."

After 1...b5 White had to retreat by 2.Qc2 remaining a solid pawn down since 2.Nxb5? is refuted by 2...Bd7! snaring a piece.

EASY DOES IT!
White sacrificed a pawn for longterm pressure. He dominates
d6 and hinders Black from developing his queenside. What next?

SYDOR - GIPSLIS
Lublin, 1969

92. White moves
(a) g4 (b) Rad1

(a) The nature of White's compensation for the pawn is gradual
pressure along the central files. Simply 1.Rad1 brings a new
rook into play and turns the screws on the backward pawn at
d7.

(b) White got impatient, fearing his advantage would evaporate
unless he aimed at the king. But there isn't enough force to do
any real damage over there. After 1.g4? Nb4!; 2.Bxf5 Nd5! (not
2...exf5; 3.Qb3+) 3.Be5 g6; 4.Qg2 Bf6 exposed the weakness of
White's kingside and the game soon turned in Black's favor.

ENDGAME CATASTROPHE

Launching an all-out offensive without sufficient force to back it up is a major error. But ignoring a threat against one of your own men by countering with an attack against an enemy man can be hazardous to your health unless it's timed right.

LASKER - EUWE
Nottingham, 1936

93. Black moves
(a) Nb6 (b) Ba5

(a) Considering the utter simplicity of the position, they could agree to a draw right now because it's hard to see how either side can make progress after 1...Nb6.

(b) 1...Ba5? lost a piece after 2.b4! Bxb4; 3.Nc2 with a double attack against the knight and bishop. The loss of this half point cost Euwe a tie for first with Botvinnik and Capabanca.

In the tournament book Alekhine wrote: "1...Ba5?? is hard indeed to understand, as even the answers 2.Nc2 or 2.Kxc4 Bxe1; 3.Be3 would yield Black no advantage. That the draw was not declared here was only, I presume, because neither player offered one. Dr. Emanuel Lasker because (although he doubtless was perfectly aware that his isolated pawn is by no means a serious weakness) he was, theoretically at least, at a slight disadvantage; Dr. Max Euwe because as the new World Champion he felt obliged to exploit even the shade of a winning chance. The unfortunate result was the ensuing catastrophe, which changed the normal course of the tournament."

SELLING TOO CHEAPLY

Although Black is a piece ahead, his queen is trapped behind enemy lines. His task is to gather as much material as possible in return for the doomed queen.

KORCHNOI - NIETO
Spain, 1998

94. Black moves
(a) b6 (b) Nd7

(a) To meet the threat of Ra3 Black should try to drive the bishop off the a3-f8 diagonal with 1...b6! (if 1...b5; 2.Rfc1) inviting 2.Bxf8 Kxf8 and the queen escapes by capturing the pawn on b4. If 2.Bd6 Rd8; 3.Ra3 Qxa3; 4.bxa3 Rxd6 gives Black a rook and two minor pieces in return for the queen, a decisive edge.

(b) Instead Black attacked the bishop prematurely by 1...Nd7?; 2.Ra3 Nxc5; 3.Rxb3 Nxb3; 4.Qd3 e5; 5.Qxb3 and got only a bishop and rook for the queen, which is inadequate. However, the following position was reached after the time control at move 40 when Korchnoi, still moving fast, made one of the worst blunders of his long career.

FINAL BLIND SPOT

The clock forces error. Tournament players often must move so fast to beat the clock that they lack time to keep score or write down moves, so they can't tell if they already made the time control and keep moving to eliminate any possible forfeit on time. This type of blunder will become more prevalent as limits get faster and faster, especially under sudden death controls which aim to finish all games in a single session.

KORCHNOI - NIETO
Spain 1998

95. White moves
(a) Qf6 (b) hxg6

(a) White still has some winning chances after 1.Qf6 Rxh5; 2.Qxa6 Kg7; 3.Ke3 Rf5; 4.Ke4.

(b) Korchnoi, unsure whether he had glided past the time control, hurriedly played 1.hxg6? Rh2+ and resigned since the queen falls next move. Errors forced by the clock are legion, which is why for the most part they are excluded from this book.

HIDDEN RESOURCES

Black is two pawns ahead and should have no trouble transforming such a huge material advantage into victory. It's just a matter of technique, isn't it?

SVESHNIKOV - SERMEK
Nova Gorica, 1998

96. Black moves
(a) Rc4 (b) Kg6

(a) After 1...Rc4 guarding the pawn Black will reach an easy book win by ...Kg6 followed by f5.

(b) Black carelessly transposed moves by 1...Kg6? first, expecting to play f5 next when the rook moves away. However, this premature attack on the rook was punished by 1.Rg5+! Kxg5 (or 1...Kf6; 2.Rxg4 is a book draw) stalemate!

MIRAGES

Attacks against the king have a good chance to succeed if there is sufficient force to back them up. Here White has a rook, queen and bishop aimed at his majesty but the fortress is hard to crack.

FISCHER - LARSEN
Santa Monica, 1963

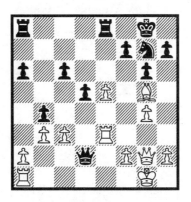

97. White moves
(a) f3 (b) Qh3

(a) White should aim for a draw by 1.f3! bxc3; 2.Qxd2 cxd2; 3.Rd1 regaining the pawn.

(b) Instead Fischer pursued a mirage by 1.Qh3? "The decisive mistake. I do not know what Fischer overlooked, but it must have been something simple," wrote Larsen. After 1...bxc3; 2.Qh6 Ne6 White resigned when he saw the simple defense 3.Bf6 c2; 4.Qxh7+ Kxh7; 5.Rh3+ Qh6! Fischer probably forgot that the queen could interpose on this square when he embarked on his misguided adventure.

OFF-DAYS
Time and again even experienced masters fall into stock opening traps. They should know better but things can go wrong in the heat of battle. This position arises from the Slav Defense: 1.d4 d5; 2.c4 c6; 3.Nf3 dxc4; 4.e3 Nf6; 5.Bxc4 Nbd7; 6.0-0 Nb6; 7.Bb3.

EVANS - STRAUSS
Los Angeles, 1963

98. Black moves
(a) Bg4 (b) Bf5

(a) Black already misplaced his knight on b6 and now compounded the error by bringing out his bishop too soon: 1...Bg4?; 2.Bxf7+! Kxf7; 3.Ne5+ Ke8; 4.Nxg4 winning a pawn by the fork.

(b) If Black doesn't want to hem in the bishop with ...e6, then a good alternative is 7...Bf5; 8.Nc3 e6.

CLEARING LINES

Failing to prosecute a mating attack without first opening lines for your forces is one of the worst sins a player can commit. It even happens at the highest level.

KARPOV - ANAND
Wijk aan Zee, 1998

99. Black moves
(a) Ra2 (b) e3

(a) The game was only drawn after 1...Ra2?; 2.Rfh2 Rxe2; 3.Rxe2 Bxe2; 4.Rxh7+ Kxh7; 5.Qxe2 Qxg3+; 6.Kd4 Qxf4; 7.Qh5+ Kg7; 8.Qe8 e3+; 9.Kd3 Qf5+; 10.Kxe3 Qxe5+;11.Kd3 because Black's king is too exposed to make any real headway.

(b) Black missed a decisive attack by first clearing lines for the queen: 1...e3!; 2.Rfh2 Ra3+; 3.Kb2 Ra2+!; 4.Kxa2 Qc2+; 5.Ka1 Ra7 mate.

SURPRISING FINALE

Clearly Black is not long for this world. All White has to do is find the right place to put his bishop and threaten Rxh7 mate.

MENGARINI - EVANS
New York State Championship, 1947

100. Black moves
(a) Be6 (b) Bc4

(a) White was getting short of time and saw that 1.Bd5 (or Bxg6) is refuted by 1...Nh3+; 2.Kh1 Rf1 mate. He missed a winning line with 1.Be6! Nh3+; 2.Bxh3 Rb1+; 3.Bf1! R8xf1+; 4.Kg2 and I would have no good defense against Rxh7+.

(b) It's only a draw after 1.Bc4? Nh3+; 2.Kh1 Nf2+; 3.Kg1 Nh3+; 4.Kh1 Nf2+. But White suddenly got the bright idea of trying to win with 5.Kg2 Ne4+; 6.Kh3? Ng5+; 7.Kg4 Rxh2! and threw it all away by 8.Bd5 (not 8.Kxg5? Rf5+; 9.Kg4 h5 mate) 8...h6; 9.a4 Rb2; 10.Kh4? Rb4+; 11.g4 Rxa4; 12.Re5 Nh7; 13.Re6 Nf6; 14.Bf3 Ra3; 15.g5 Rxf3. White resigns.

COFFEE-HOUSE ATTACKS

Before making a move always assume your opponent will find the right reply and prepare a sensible follow-up. But sometimes it's hard to resist going after a tempting target when there's a lot to gain and not much to lose.

LOVAS - ASZTALOS
Budapest, 1915

101. White moves
(a) h3 (b) Ng5

(a) Objectively speaking, White has no reason to assume the time is ripe to launch an attack while his heavy pieces are unable to support the fray. The calm 1.h3 not only creates an escape square for the bishop or king at h2 but also, in some cases, prepares g4.

(b) Instead White advanced an already developed piece by 1.Ng5!? attacking the pawn at h7 which can be readily defended with 1...g6 and White has no effective follow-up. But Black fell into a trap by 1...h6? and lost beautifully after 2.Bh7+ Kf8; 3.Ng6+! fxg6; 4.Nxe6+ Kf7; 5.Qxg6+ Kxe6; 6.Bg8+ Kd7; 7.Qf5 mate.

The success of these flashy attacks depends upon the unwitting cooperation of a weaker adversary who doesn't see what's coming. That's why it's called coffee-house chess.

HOT WATER

"Despite a century of opening analysis it's amazing how much hot water a master can wade into in the first dozen moves," observed Napier. This brevity arose from a standard sequence in the English Opening: 1.c4 e5; 2.Nc3 Nf6; 3.Nf3 Nc6; 4.g3 Bb4; 5.Nd5.

PETROSIAN - REE
Wijk aan Zee, 1971

102. Black moves
(a) Nxd5 (b) Bc5

(a) Too dangerous is 1...Nxd5; 2.cxd5 e4? (it's better go give up a pawn by 2...Nd4; 3.Nxe5 Qe7; 4.f4) 3.dxc6 exf3; 4.Qb3! and Black resigned because he must drop a piece after 4...fxe2; 5.Bxe2 Qe7; 6.a3 Bc5; 7.cxb7.

(b) A hard game lies ahead after 1...Bc5; 2.d3 h6 (to stop the pin by Bg5) 3.Bg2 0-0; 4.a3 Re8!; 5.b4 Bf8 (tucking in the bishop) 6.Bb2 d6.

FOOLS RUSH IN

White has laid a diabolical trap but Black is oblivious. This can happen if you get too preoccupied with your own schemes and underestimate the opponent's resources.

MIESES - WOLF
Monte Carlo, 1903

103. Black moves
(a) Nf4 (b) Kb8

(a) Black rushed in to threaten mate with 1...Nf4? but was knocked off his seat by 2.Nb6+! axb6; 3.Qa8 mate.

(b) The best defense is 1...Kb8; 2.Rc5 Qf7. Now if 3.Ra5 Rhd8; 4.Nc5 Rd1 offers Black just enough counterplay to hold his own.

FLANK ATTACKS

Black is a pawn ahead. He must decide whether to break the pin or secure the center.

ROSENTRETER - HOFER
Berlin, 1899

104. Black moves
(a) d6 (b) g5

(a) Generally it's a good idea to secure the center before embarking on a wing attack, especially when your king hasn't yet castled. Correct is 1...d6; 2.f4 Qe7 to pave the way for queenside castling. It's better to accept doubled pawns by 3.fxe5 dxe5; 4.Bxf6 gxf6 than to tarry with the king in the center.

(b) Black figured he had time for 1...g5? driving the bishop back but had to throw in the towel after 2.f4! gxf4; 3.Rxf4! exf4; 4.Qxd4 0-0; 5.Bxf6 Qe8; 6.Bh8.

Moral: Batten down the hatches before attacking on a flank.

NO TURNING BACK
One bad move leads to another. Once you are caught up in this ugly sequence, there's no way out.

BOTVINNIK - SPIELMANN
Moscow, 1935

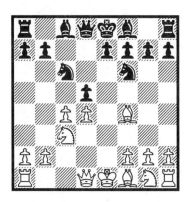

105. Black moves
(a) e6 (b) Qb6

(a) The safest continuation is 1...e6; 2.Nf3 Be7 (or dxc4).

(b) A Viennese millionaire is reputed to have left a fortune to his nephew on the sole condition that the lad never capture a pawn on b2 with his queen.

Black threw caution to the winds with 1...Qb6? It might work against a weak player but violates principle by bringing the queen out too early. The game ended quickly after 2.cxd5 Qxb2 (taking the plunge; also bad is 2...Nxd4; 3.Be3) 3.Rc1 Nb4; 4.Na4 Qxa2 (or 4...Qa3; 5.Rc3 Qxa2; 6.Bc4) 5.Bc4 Qa3; 6 Rc3.

Chapter 6

MISCALCULATION

"I see one move ahead. The best one." — Jose Capablanca

Many players are so busy hatching their own plots that they seldom pay attention to what their opponent is doing — until it's too late. There's an easy way to overcome this fault if you stick to it: EVERY TIME YOUR OPPONENT MAKES A MOVE FORGET YOUR OWN PLANS FOR A MOMENT AND ASK YOURSELF, "WHAT DOES HE THREATEN?"

Look at his last move. Why did he make it? Does it attack or endanger one of your men? Look at his other pieces, even if they seem far removed from the scene of action. Has his move created a secondary threat and can it be ignored? Finally, is your king still safe?

Eventually you will be able to assess any move in a matter of seconds. After all, everything is open and above-board. The element of deception is at a minimum and there are no closed hands, as in bridge.

Capablanca said that he had to lose hundreds of games before he got good. Rapid and accurate calculation was the most essential tool in his kit. Visualization — the ability to see ahead and evaluate positions in your mind's eye without touching pieces — can be trained with practice and more practice. You can start by studying this book strictly from the diagram without a board.

The danger in trying to see too far ahead is that it's quite easy to miss something along the way. There's an old saying, "Long analysis, wrong analysis." Frequently all you have to do is ask yourself, "If I make this move, what will be his best reply? What do I do then, and who will stand better?"

BEYOND THE HORIZON
The number of moves a chess computer can see ahead is known as its horizon. Machines are programmed to search ahead a fixed number of plies (half-moves), and they can't see over the rainbow. This limitation explains some of the silly mistakes that crop up from time to time.

When a microcomputer can search ahead 4-ply (four half moves) this translates into two full moves by White and Black. A good example of the horizon effect took place at an early computer tournament after 1.d4 d5; 2.Nc3 Nc6; 3.Bf4 Bf5; 4.e3 e6; 5.h4.

BORIS DIPLOMAT - VOICE SENSORY CHALLENGER
Computer Match, 1981

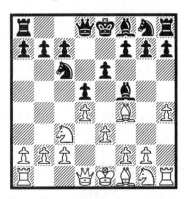

106. Black moves
(a) Nf6 (c) Bb4

(a) Most humans would assume the sole purpose of White's last move was to trap the bishop with g4. 1...Nf6 develops the knight to a good square and stops g4 cold.

(b) The machine chose 1...Bb4? which cost a piece after 2.g4 Bxc3+; 3.bxc3 Be4; 4.f3 Bg6; 5.h5. Why didn't it see this coming? When considering 1...Bb4 the program searched all legal replies including, of course, 2 g4. It knew that such a pawn advance is inferior because it exposes the kingside, so the only good reason for it would be to snare the bishop. But how far ahead is poor Black supposed to look? It's already at four-ply after 1...Bxc3+; 2.bxc3 Be4 and material is still level, ergo it concluded there's nothing to fear from 2.g4.

THE HUMAN HORIZON
White tried one last gasp before resigning. It succeeded beyond his wildest expectations!

OLTE - NICHOLS
Connecticut, 1974

107. White moves
(a) hxg3 (b) h4

(a) Both moves lose — don't get me wrong — but there is no chance for a miracle after 1.hxg3 gxf5 followed by Kxg3. Equally hopeless is 1.fxg6 gxh2.

(b) Might as well try 1.h4 since the alternatives are hopeless. So what was Black's response? He resigned! Dumbfounded, White had the wherewithal to ask if Black was, in fact, resigning. Black said yes because he didn't see a way to stop White from queening his pawn.

True — except for one not so insignificant detail: 1...g2+; 2.Kg1 gxf5; 3.h5 Kg3; 4.h6 f3; 5.h8/Q f2 mate!

This is a practical example of the "horizon effect" on a human, the analysis of a given position after a prescribed number of moves without taking into account the very next move at the end of your analysis. Apparently it was beyond the ability of Black, who was rated 1750, to see so far ahead. So he gave up.

WRONG RECAPTURE
White just played 1 dxe5 swapping pawns. Black has two ways to recapture, and there is a vast difference between them.

EVANS - JOYNER
Canadian Open, 1956

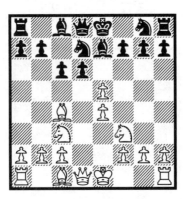

108. Black moves
(a) Nxe5   (b) dxe5

(a) Eager to relieve his cramp, Black selected 1...Nxe5? but failed to reckon one move beyond the horizon. He resigned in disgust after 2.Nxe5 dxe5; 3.Qh5! g6; 4.Qxe5 f6; 5.Qg3 Qd4; 6.Bb3 Bd6; 7.Bf4 Bxf4; 8.Qxf4 Qe5; 9.Qe3 Ne7; 10.0-0-0.

(b) Black should be in no hurry to simplify. After 1...dxe5 I intended 2.Ng5 Bxg5; 3.Qh5 Ngf6; 4.Qxg5 enjoying the slight advantage of two bishops, but a long struggle lies ahead.

A SIMPLE ENDGAME

Many king and pawn endgames look simple because there are so few pieces on the board. Chess is reduced to bare mathematics when both sides have passed pawns that can queen, so all you have to do is count moves to see who gets there first. But you also must look ahead at what happens after both sides queen, and this requires foresight and imagination in addition to mere calculation.

LUBOYEVIC - BROWNE
Amsterdam, 1972

109. Black moves
(a) f5 (b) Kd5

(a) One move wins — the other only draws. Not suspecting he had anything, Black drew by 1...f5?; 2.Kb4 f4; 3.Kc3 f3; 4.Kd2 f2; 5.Ke2. The White king is said to be "within the square" since it gets back in four moves when it takes five moves for the pawn to queen.

(b) In the endgame the king is a fighting piece — use it! This placid setting lulled Black into thinking there was nothing beneath the surface. He probably never considered the paradoxical 1...Kd5! because it looks so silly. In fact, it even permits White to queen first! But Black nevertheless wins after 2.b4 (if 2.Kb4 Kd4!; 3.Ka3 f5; 4.Kb2 f4; 5.Kc1 Ke3; 6.Kd1 Kf2!; 7.b4 f3; 8.b5 Kg2; 9.b6 f2; 10.b7 f1/Q with check) 2...f5; 3.b5 f4; 4.b6 Kc6!; 5.Ka6 f3; 6.b7 f2; 7.b8/Q f1/Q+; 8.Ka5 Qa1+; 9.Kb4 Qb1+; 10.Kc3 Qxb8.

THE LAST LAUGH

You can ignore a threat only if you have a more potent one of your own. Here a neat twist enabled me to get the last laugh.

BISGUIER - EVANS
USA Championship, 1957

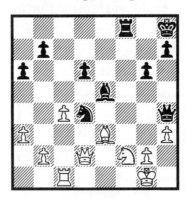

110. White moves
(a) Ng4 (b) Rd1

(a) White is under pressure, facing the immediate threat of Nb3. Bisguier thought he found a solution with 1.Ng4? Nb3; 2.Qe1 which seems to force a queen swap after 2...Qxe1+; 3.Rxe1 and if now 3...Bxb2?; 4.Rb1. Or 2...Bg3?; 3.Qc3+ Kg8; 4.Qxb3. However, he overlooked that 2...Nxc1! wins the exchange because of the back rank mate ensuing after 3.Qxh4 Ne2+; 4.Kh1 Rf1. So he had to settle for 3.Qxc1 Bg7 when Black's win became a matter of technique.

(b) One careless rook move can lead to disaster: e.g., 1.Rf1? Nf3+!; 2.gxf3 Qg3+; 3.Kh1 Qh2 mate. White can avert material loss by 1.Rd1! Nf5 (unsound is 1...Qg3?; 2.Bxd4 Qh2+; 3.Kf1 Qh1+; 4.Ke2) 2.b3! h5 (if 2...Qg3; 3.Ng4) 3.Nh1! which looks ugly but holds.

SLIPSHOD ANALYSIS

Stopping your analysis too soon is by far the most common type of miscalculation. You see ahead for a few moves and then misjudge the resulting position, as in this example.

EVANS - HOROWITZ
USA Championship, 1951

111. Black moves
(a) Qe4 (b) Rg3

(a) White's passed pawn is more dangerous than Black's passed pawn because it is further advanced, but it doesn't confer a decisive advantage. The simplest solution is 1...Qe4!; 2.Qxe4 dxe4; 3.c7 Rc8; 4.Kg2 Kg7; 5.Kg3 Kf6; 6.Kf4 Ke7; 7.Kxe4 Kd7; 8.Kf5 Rxc7; 9.Rxc7+ Kxc7; 10.Kg5 Kd6; 11.Kh6 Ke7; 12.Kxh7 Kf8 with a well-known draw (13.h4 Kf7; 14.h5 Kf8; 15.h6 Kf7; 16.Kh8 Kf8; 17.h7 stalemate).

(b) Black opted for 1...Rg3? expecting to draw by repetition with 2.Qf8+ Rg8; 3.Qf3, etc. But now 2.c7! Rxf3 (Black runs out of checks after 2...Rxh3+; 3.Qxh3 Qe4+; 4.Qg2 Qh4+; 5. Kg1 Qd4+; 6.Qf2 Qg4+; 7.Kf1 Qh3+; 8.Ke1 Qe6+; 9.Qe2) 2.c8/ Q+ Kg7; 3.Qg4+ picks up the rook and the game — yet another example of a player failing to see beyond the horizon.

AMBUSHED

Seeing ahead — but not far enough — is the sin of an advanced beginner. We all know that a little knowledge can be a dangerous thing. This accounts for a fetching trap that seems to exploit a pin in the Queen's Gambit Declined after 1.d4 d5; 2.c4 e6; 3.Nc3 Nf6; 4.Bg5 Nbd7; 5.cxd5 exd5.

112. White moves
(a) Nxd5 (b) e3

(a) White released the central tension by swapping pawns but now got a brainstorm with 1.Nxd5? figuring that 1...Nxd5 is impossible in view of 2.Bxd8. This is fine as far as it goes, but it doesn't go far enough. White stopped analzying too soon without taking into account an ambush at the tail end of the pin. The hole in his "analysis" is 2...Bb4+!; 3.Qd2 (forced) Bxd2+; 4.Kxd2 Kxd8 emerging a knight ahead.

(b) After 1.e3 Be7 (now Nxd5 was really threatened) 2.Bd3 the game continues normally and White can decide later whether to castle kingside or queenside. It's a good idea to keep your opponent guessing about where your pieces will go.

PROCESS OF ELIMINATION
Errors occur even in simple settings because players get confused when confronted with a choice between two moves. If both moves look bad, try to eliminate the one which looks worse!

MARCHAND - EVANS
Lone Pine, 1971

113. White moves
(a) Kd3 (b) Kc1

(a) After 1.Kd3? e2; 2.Rf6 (White must lose a tempo defending his pawn) 2...Kd1; 3.Ra6 Rh3+. White resigned.

(b) The only chance to draw is 1.Kc1! e2 (1...Ke2; 2.Rf6 Kd3; 3.Rd6+ Ke4; 4.Kd1 holds) 2.Rf6 Rh1; 3.Kc2 and it's not clear how Black can free his king to make progress.

GIFT OF THE GODS
Nowadays, faster time limits force games to be finished in a single session. This is a good idea because it throws both sides entirely on their own resources and eliminates adjournments when friends and computers can be consulted overnight.

I was on the USA team at the Haifa Olympiad in 1976 that brought the gold medal back to America after a hiatus of 39 years. Our secret weapon was accurate analysis of adjourned games. In all, 18 out of our 52 games were unfinished. We calculated that with correct play the result should have been 9-9. Our actual tally was 13 1/2 - 4 1/2!

I had Black in six out of nine games yet posted the best overall score in the entire Olympiad: 83.3% (6 wins, 3 draws). This ending was typical of my good fortune. When awakened by the team captain in the morning, my intention was to go in and agree to a draw, sign the scoresheet and go back to sleep. To my surprise, Lombard was sitting deep in thought studying the position after my sealed move was revealed on the board. Why was he taking so long? Didn't the Swiss team analyze the position overnight?

EVANS - LOMBARD
Haifa Olympiad, 1976

114. Black moves
(a) Rh1+   (b) Kf3

(a) Black can draw easily by 1...Rh1+; 2.Ke2 (not 2.Kc2? e2) 2...Rh2+; 3.Kd3 Rd2+; 4.Kc4 e2; 5.Re8 Rxb2.

(b) Apparently my sealed move was unexpected. Black lost a tempo by 1...Kf3?; 2.Rf8+ Ke4; 3.Re8+ Kd3; 4.Rd8+ Ke4; 5.b4 Ra2; 6.a5 e2+; 7.Ke1 Ke3; 8.Re8+ Kf3; 9.c4 Ra4 (White's pawns are too menacing after 9...Ra1+; 10.Kd2 Rd1+; 11.Kc3 e1/Q+; 12.Rxe1 Rxe1; 13.a6) 10.Rxe2 Rxb4; 11.Re6 Rxc4; 12.Kd2 Kf4; 13.a6. It was adjourned again and analysis showed that White wins by a tempo. The conclusion: 13...Kf5; 14.Re8! Ra4; 15.Ra8 Kf6; 16.Kc3 Ra1; 17.Kb4 Rb1+; 18.Kc5 Rc1+; 19.Kb6 Rb1+; 20.Ka7 Ke7; 21.Rb8 Rc1; 22.Rb2 Rc3; 23.Kb8. Black resigns.

OVER-OPTIMISM

I just escaped from a ticklish predicament and was feeling pretty good despite the fact that my king is in check. After all, White has to meet the mate threat of Qa1+ (and also Qxd5) doesn't he?

GUIMARD - EVANS
Buenos Aires, 1960

115. Black moves
(a) Bxh6 (b) Kg7

(a) I captured the knight without too much thought but didn't see far enough ahead. After 1...Bxh6?; 2.Qe8+ Kh7; 3.Qxf7+ Bg7; 4.Be4+ Kh6 my king looked safe because White has no more checks. However 4.Qf5! Qa1+; 5.Bb1 e4; 6.Qxe4 not only stops the back rank mate but also renews the devastating threat of Qh7 mate. I had to give up.

(b) After the prudent 1...Kg7! (not 1...Kh7; 2.Be4+) 2.Nf5+ Kh7 White finally must deal with the double threat of Qa1+ or Qxd5.

FIGHTING FOR THE CENTER

White's pawn on e4 is under fire. Should he push it or leave it there and maintain the tension?

SMITH - EVANS
Santa Monica, 1964

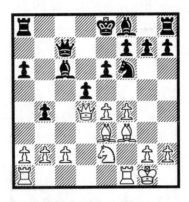

116. White moves
(a) Ng3   (b) e5

(a) Anything is better than 1.Ng3? dxe4; 2.Nxe4 Bxe4! and White resigned in view of 3.Bxe4 Rd8 netting material after 3.Qb6 Qxb6; 4.Bxb6 Nxe4; 5.Bxd8 Bc5+; 6.Kh1 Kxd8.

(b) It's still anybody's game after 1.e5 Nd7. Even 1.exd5 Bxd5; 2.Rac1 is playable in a pinch.

THE WRONG TARGET
White's attack is so overwhelming that it looks as if any old move will win. But there is always a way to go wrong.

RADOICIC - EVANS
USA Open, 1955

117. White moves
(a) Qf7+ (b) Re3

(a) I was ready to resign after 1.Qf7+ Kh8; 2.Qxg6 (or 2.Rf6).

(b) As we saw so many times, one bad move leads to another. White fixated on the queen instead of the king and interpolated 1.Re3!? giving me a chance to save myself with 1...Ne5! White can still win with 2.Rxe5! Qxe5; 3.Qf7+ Kh8; 4.Qxg6 but, short of time, nabbed the queen and lost after 2.Rxc3? bxc3; 3.Nc7?! Nc4! (threatening Na3 mate) 4.a4 Rf8; 5.Nxa8 Rxf2 and White resigns.

A QUIET MIRACLE

White is winning but can't queen the pawn right away without getting mated. "Chess miracles, as opposed to the other sort, still happen on occasion, thanks to players' fantasies and the game's endless possibilities," noted Bronstein.

SMYSLOV - PETROSIAN
Zurich, 1953

118. White moves
(a) Qxd3+ (b) Qd6

(a) On 1.d8/Q? Qf4+; 2.Kh3 (or 2.Kh5 g6 mate) 2...Nf2 mate. "Convinced that a genuine miracle had come to pass, Smyslov resigned himself to the loss of a half point and forced the draw with a sham queen sacrifice by 1.Qxd3+ cxd3; 2.d8/Q. In turn, Black's attempt to play for the win would be easily rebuffed: 2...Qe2; 3.Kh3 d2; 4.Qd7 d1/Q; 5.Qf5+." (Bronstein)

(b) "However, as it turns out, miracles are sometimes no more than optical illusions in chess as well. On 1.Qd6! Nf2+; 2.Kh4 g5+; 3.Kh5 wins; and on any other Black reply, White simply makes another queen and his king easily escapes the checks. Curiously, neither player, nor the tournament participants, nor the spectators, noticed this possibility for White. 1.Qd6! was discovered by a Swedish amateur some months later." (Bronstein)

DESPERATE MEASURES

Black is two pawns behind and clearly on the verge of defeat. Alas, Geller failed to find the saving resource.

RESHEVSKY - GELLER
Zurich, 1953

119. Black moves
(a) Rxa3 (b) Rb8

(a) The saving clause is based on the weakness of White's back rank. The correct defense is 1...Rxa3!; 2.b7 Rb4; 3.Rd8+ Kh7; 4.b8/Q Rxb8; 5.Rxb8 Rd3!; 6.Rf1 Rc3! Now on 7.h3 c1/Q; 8.Rxc1 Rxc1+; 9.Kh2 enters a theoretically drawn 4 vs. 3 rook and pawn ending.

(b) Instead Geller reached a lost ending after 1...Rb8?; 2.Rd6 Ra4; 3.Rxc2 Rxa3; 4.h3 Rb3; 5.R2c6 Rb2; 6.e4 h5; 7.e5 h4 but Reshevsky eventually let the win slip away after failing to find 8.e6 f6; 9.Rc7 Rxb6; 10.R6d7.

SEALED MOVES

Two moves before adjournment I refused a draw but then blundered in time pressure. To my horror I saw that Black could now win a piece if he sealed the right move.

EVANS - DRIMER
Havana Olympiad, 1966

120. Black moves
(a) Kg8 (b) Bh4+

(a) I stayed up all night trying to find a defense to 1...Kg8! nudging the overburdened rook. The line I feared was 2.Be6 Bd6+!; 3.Kf2 Re5!; 4.Re7+ (if 4.Bd5? Rxd5) 4...Kf8; 5.d4 Kxe7; 6.dxe5 Kxe6; 7.exd6 Kxd6 and Black wins the ensuing king and pawn ending by virtue of his outside passed pawn.

(b) I needed a miracle. The next morning I went in to play it off and his sealed move was 1...Bh4+? I leaped for joy, then bitterly thought of the sleep I lost fighting phantoms. Now Black had an easy draw after 2.Kf1 Kg8; 3.Be6 Re5; 4.Rf4+ Rxe6; 5.Rxh4 Rxe3; 6.Rxh6 Rxd3; 7.Rh5. Later I learned that at no time before, during, or after adjourning, did Drimer dream he could have won a piece with 1...Kg8!

BAD TIMING

It's not enough to find good moves. They must also be played in the right order.

ZITA - GOLOMBEK
Prague, 1946

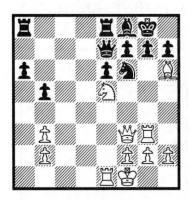

121. White moves
(a) Nc6 (b) Bg5

(a) White is a pawn down but has an overwhelming attack. He wants to play Qxf6 and figures that after 1.Nc6 Black's queen will be forced to abandon its defense of that square. However after 1...Qc7! White noticed to his chagrin that 2.Qxf6? Qxg3! refutes his plan. So the game continued 2.Re5? (the best chance now is 2.Bxg7 Bxg7; 3.Re5 Kf8; 4.Reg5) 2...g6; 3.Bxf8 Rxf8; 4.Qxf6 Qxc6 and Black's extra pawn soon prevailed.

(a) The clincher is 1.Bg5! increasing pressure on f6. If 1...Kh8; 2.Bxf6 gxf6 (or 2...Qxf6; 3.Qxf6 gxf6; 4.Nxf7 mate) and now 3.Nc6! forces the queen to abandon its defense of f6.

HE WHO HESITATES....

Many queen and pawn endings are drawn by perpetual check because it's hard to find shelter for the kings on an open board. Here material is even but White's dangerous passed pawn is only two squares away from queening.

ALEKHINE - RESHEVSKY
AVRO, 1938

122. White moves
(a) d7 (b) Qd1

(a) The world champion missed a simple win by 1.d7! Qd6; 2.Qe8 when Black can't draw by perpetual check. If 2...Qd2+; 3.Kh3 Qd1; 4.d8/Q Qf1+; 5.Kh4 g5+; 6.Kg4 f5+; 7.Kxf5 Qxf3+; 8.Ke5 and the king will find shelter on the queenside.

(b) Alekhine lost a vital tempo by 1.Qd1? Qd8; 2.d7 c4; 3.Qxa4 c3; 4.Qc6 c2; 5.Qc3+ Kh7; 6.Qxc2 Qxd7; 7.Qa2 Kg8; 8.a4 Qc6; 9.a5 Qa6 and a draw was agreed a dozen moves later when it became clear that White was unable to make progress.

KNIGHT ON THE RIM

There's an old saying, "Knight on the rim equals trim." But every rule has exceptions.

BOGOLJUBOV - FLOHR
Nottingham, 1936

123. White moves
(a) Nf3 (b) Nh7

(a) This position is no exception. A draw would be likely after the prudent 1.Nf3 e5; 2 g5.

(b) The double attack on f6 seems to justify the decentralization of the knight, but actually it cost White the exchange and also the game after 1.Nh7? Rh8!; 2.Rxf6 (White probably intended 2.Nxf6 Rh3+; 3.Kf2 Kxf6; 4.Kg2+ followed by Kxh3, but missed the zwischenzug 3...Bb5!) 2...Be8; 3.Rxg6 Bxg6; 4.Ng5 Rh4.

PHOTO FINISH

Certain positions look so good that any move seems to win. But sometimes a little trick makes a big difference.

GUFELD - BRONSTEIN
USSR, 1968

124. White moves
(a) Kf7 (b) Kg7

(a) Let us turn to Gufeld's description of what happened: "I had to seal a move. I quickly wrote down 1.Kf7 on my scoresheet. Afterwards it would turn out that this particular move would have won very easily...." White's king needs to cross over to the queenside to support the advance of the c-pawn.

(b) "But then I thought it over again and decided on something stronger, so I changed my sealed move to 1.Kg7. Later a curious conversation between Bronstein and me took place. 'Which move did you write down 1.Kf7 or 1.Kg7?' asked the amiable David Ionovich. I replied that from my point of view it made no difference. Bronstein smiled craftily and said, 'If 1.Kg7 is the sealed move then an unpleasant surprise awaits you. I will play 1...Kg4 and after 2.Rd4+ Kh5; 3.c4 Rxc4! there is stalemate.' My face fell."

Gufeld varied but it was drawn anyway after 1.Kg7? Kg4; 2.Rh2 Kg3; 3.Rh1 Rxc2; 4.h5 Rc7+; 5.Kf6 Rc6+; 6.Ke5 Rh6; 7.Ke4 Kg2!; 8.Rh4 Kg3.

COSTLY TRANSPOSITIONS
Reversing the order of moves can be costly. Here's more proof if proof be needed.

SVESHNIKOV - FERCEC
Nova Gorica, 1998

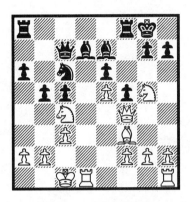

125. White moves
(a) Nb6 (b) Rxd7

(a) Black is hard-pressed to find a good defense against 1.Nb6! If 1...Qxb6; 2.Rxd7 Bxg5; 3.Qxg5 Rf7; 4.Rd6 is decisive. Or 1...Qxe5; 2.Qxe5 Bxg5+; 3.Qe3 Bxe3+; 4.fxe3 gains material.

(b) Instead White transposed moves with 1.Rxd7? Qxd7 and suddenly saw that his intended 2.Nb6 Qd8; 3.Nxa8 Bxg5 costs his queen. The game continued 2.Rd1 Bxg5; 3.Qxg5 Qc7; 4.Na5? Nxa5; 5.Bxa8 Rxa8 and Black's extra material prevailed.

Chapter 7

IMPULSIVENESS

"When you see a good move, look for a better one!"
— Chess Adage

One of my students described a familiar ailment that is easy to diagnose but hard to cure: "The biggest obstacle I must overcome is jumping at the first move I see, not taking into account any forks or combinative play that my opponent may have planned."

The itch to move is hard to resist, especially in tournament games with the clock ticking relentlessly. There is only one proven remedy: sit on your hands!

SECOND THOUGHTS

In an era when time limits are getting faster and faster, you no longer have the luxury of long thinks. When you see a good move, maybe you should make it!

EVANS-BENKO
Las Vegas, 1966

126. White to move
(a) P-N4+   (b) P-R3

(a) I rapidly calculated that 1.g4+! hxg4; 2.hxg4+ Kxg4; 3.Ke4 wins by force. White is temporarily a pawn down but Black's king has been deflected and the rest is a matter of simple arithmetic: 3...Kg3; 4.Kxe5 Kf3; 5.Kd5 Ke3; 6.Kc5 Kd3; 7.Kxb5 Kc2; 8.Kxc4 Kxb2; 9.a4 Kb3; 10.Kb5 Kxc3; 11.Kxa5 and the pawn will queen.

But there is a human element to chess, and this game illustrates the devastating effect that time pressure can have — on your opponent! Benko had two seconds to reach the time control and I had a good half hour. Unfortunately I had time to think, and it cost me first prize.

(b) The win slipped through my fingers because it was too simple! Not content with finding it, I somehow convinced myself there was no need to rush things. Since g4 isn't going to run away, why not first strengthen my position by anchoring the king on e4? Suddenly I glanced at the clock and it seemed like I, rather than Benko, was short of time. So I impetuously played 1.a3? expecting 1...a4 whereupon I could then play 2.g4+ and arrive at the winning line.

But I had to agree to a draw after 1.a3? Kf6!; 2.Ke4 Ke6; 3.Ke3 Kf6. Drat! The win evaporated because I forgot Black doesn't have to return his king to f5. I suddenly saw, to my grief, that 4.g4? is refuted by 4...h4! (since it's no longer check, Black doesn't have to capture) 5.Kf2 Kg5; 6.Kg2 e4!; 7.fxe4 Kxg4 and now Black's outside passed pawn prevails.

GILDING THE LILY
White is a pawn ahead and on the verge of victory. In addition, Black is all tied up. What can possibly go wrong?

LEVENFISH - CHEKHOVER
Moscow, 1935

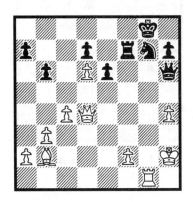

127. White moves
(a) Rxg7+ (b) b4

(a) As in the previous example, White saw the win by 1.Rxg7+ Rxg7; 2.Qxg7+ Qxg7; 3.Bxg7 Kxg7; 4.Kg3 Kf6; 5.Kf4 e5+; 6.Ke4 Ke6; 7.h5! Kxd6; 8.Kf5. But he wasn't entirely sure of his calculations and stalled for time to determine if his calculations were correct.

(b) What happened next was curious but not unusual. The pin won't run away, White figured, so why bother embarking on a wholesale series of exchanges at g7? His overfinesse with 1.b4? met with a stunning rebuke in 1...e5! when the overburdened queen can no longer protect both f2 and h4. After 2.Rxg7+!? Qxg7 White played on for a few more moves before resigning. "Whom the gods would destroy, they first make mad," he said after the game was over.

FROZEN IN HORROR

Have you ever moved too fast and then realized it was a mistake while waiting for your opponent to pounce on it? I experienced such a moment of horror and would have given anything to take back my last move. But it was too late.

EVANS - SUTTLES
San Antonio, 1962

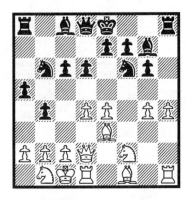

128. White moves
(a) g5 (b) Be2

(a) Black threatens to win a pawn with Nxg4 and I was reluctant to let him ease the cramp by swapping a piece after 1.g5 Ng4 but as it turns out this was the proper course.

(b) I played 1.Be2 but instantly saw the refutation. Black's reply wasn't long in coming: 1...Nxg4!; 2.Nxg4 Bxg4 winning a pawn (if 3.Bxg4 Nc4; 4.Qe2 Nxe3; 5.Qxe3? Bh6 is the quietus). I sought to obtain counterplay with 3 Rag1 but in the long run couldn't overcome the material deficit.

KIDDING YOURSELF

"Fischer doesn't always make the best move," said one of his rivals. "But he always makes a good one." The main reason you move too fast is kidding yourself that it's the best move. Here White sacked a piece, thinking he could either win a queen or checkmate.

GOMPERT - EVANS
New York, 1947

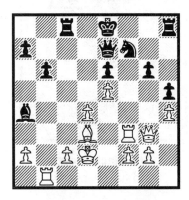

129. White moves
(a) Bxg6 (b) Rxf7

(a) White has at least a draw by 1.Bxg6 Rf8; 2.Bxf7+ Rxf7; 3.Qg8+ Rf8; 4.Rxf8+ Qxf8; 5.Qxe6+ Kd8; 6.Qd5+ Ke8; 7.Qe6+ Kd8 etc.

(b) Instead White chose 1.Rxf7? Kxf7! (he thought 1...Qxf7; 2.Bxg6 was forced) 2.Qxg6+ Kf8 and had to resign since he is now a whole rook behind. He simply saw a mate that wasn't there and overlooked the escape square at f8.

A DROP OF POISON

Black is a pawn behind and can regain it to reach an even ending. But there is a drop of poison.

EVANS - KRAMER
New York, 1954

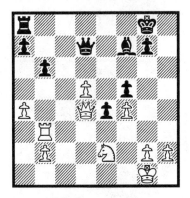

130. Black moves
(a) Bxd5 (b) Qxd5

(a) Both moves regain the pawn, and both look equally attractive. But the correct one is 1...Bxd5! and if 2.Rc3 Be6, is equal.

(b) 1...Qxd5?; 2.Rg3! Qxd4+; 3.Nxd4 snares a pawn. The rest, though tough, merely required precision: 3...Rd8; 4.Nxf5 Rd1+; 5.Kf2 Rd2+; 6.Ke3 Rxb2; 7.Kxe4 Rb4+; 8.Ke5 g6; 9.Ne7+ Kg7; 10.Nxg6! Rxa4; 11.Ne7+ Kf8; 12.Nf5 Rc4; 13.Rd3 Rc5+; 14.Kf6 Rc6+; 15.Rd6 Rxd6+; 16.Nxd6 a5; 17.Nxf7 a4; 18.Nd8! a3; 19.Ne6+ Ke8; 20.Nd4 a2; 21.Nb3. Black resigns.

LOOK BEFORE YOU LEAP

Since you can't retract a bad move, the best way to guard against an impetuous decision is to double check your analysis before you err. The moving finger writes, and having writ moves on....

EVANS - WEXLER
Buenos Aires, 1960

131. White moves
(a) Nb6 (b) Na3

(a) I thought Black's last move (Rb8c8) was unplayable because of the knight fork on b6. So I didn't bother to look again but after 1.Nb6? Rxd6; 2.Nxc8 (too late I saw that 2.Rxd6 Rc1+; 3.Kh2 Nxd6 saves the day) 2...Rxd1+; 3.Kh2 Rd5; 4.Kg3 Rc5; 5.Nb6 Nf6 I resigned in disgust.

(b) White should settle for an easy draw by 1.Na3 Rxd6; 2.Rxd6 Nxd6; 3.Nxb5 Rb8; 4.Nd4 Rxb3; 5.Nxb3, etc. But not 1.Rxb5? Rxc4; 2.Rb8 (or 2.Re1 Rc8) 2...Re4 holding the piece.

WHAT'S THE NEXT MOVE?
Sometimes you can ruin a perfectly good position by failing to ask yourself a simple question: "After I make my next move, what will be his most likely reply?" Here material is even, a draw seems imminent and neither side faces any great danger.

EVANS - RUBEL
New York, 1946

132. Black moves
(a) Rg8   (b) Ke7

(a) 1...Rg8? is the kind of move someone might flick off in a speed game, hoping for 2. Qc4? Rxg2+!; 3.Kxg2 Qg3+; 4.Kh1 Qh2 mate. Instead Black had to resign after 2.Bxe6+! Kxe6; 3.Qc4+ Ke7; 4.Qxg8.

(b) After 1...Ke7 the position is level. If 2.Qc4 Qe4 holds everything.

CASHING IN TOO SOON

A material advantage won't run away. You can cash it in slowly but surely without rushing matters, but I got impatient.

O'KELLY - EVANS
New York, 1951

133. BLACK MOVES
(a) Qe2 (b) e5

(a) A pawn ahead, I sought a quick kill by 1...Qe2? which weakens g7. The result was a draw by perpetual check after 2.Rxg7+! Kxg7; 3.Qd7+ Kf6; 4.Qd8+ Ke5; 5.Qa4+ Kd4; 6.Qb4+ Kd5 (if 6...Qc4; 7.Qxe1 is the saving clause) 7.Qa5+ Kc6; 8.Qc3+ Kb6 and my king made a Cook's Tour of the board in a vain effort to find sanctuary.

This reminds me of the old story about two coffee-house players. "If you give me another check, I'll smack you!" warned White. Black checked again and got smacked. They both landed in jail.

(b) It's hard to see how White saves himself after 1...e5! with the threat of e4 and Qf3+. Black's king can find shelter after 2.f3 Qb4; 3.Rxg7+ Kxg7; 4.Qd7+ Kf6; 5.Qc6+ Ke7; 6.Qc7+ Ke6; 7.Qc8+ Kd5 because his queen is strongly placed on b4 instead of e2. Also inadequate is 1...e5!; 2.Qf3 Rg1+ or 2.Rd3 Qe2.

STRETCHING YOUR LEGS

"Nobody can concentrate at full intensity for five uninterrupted hours. We need to stretch our legs, get some refreshment, rest the brain for a few minutes. Just remember that when you leave the board you break your concentration. When you return, take a minute or two to get your head on straight," advised Pal Benko after he came to grief in this game.

FISCHER - BENKO
Curacao, 1962

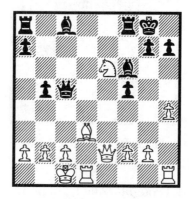

134. Black moves
(a) Bxe6   (b) Bxb2+

(a) "I pressed the clock and got up to visit the restroom. When I returned, I smiled when I saw Fischer had indeed taken my pawn on e6. Unthinkingly and before even sitting down I grabbed his knight, completely forgetting for that one moment what I had planned in case he took the poisoned pawn" lamented Benko, who lost after 1...Bxe6?; 2.Qxe6+ Kh8; 3.Kb1 Qxf2; 4.Qxf5 Qxf5; 5.Bxf5 g6 (if 5...Bxb2; 6.Be4 Rae8; 7.Bc6 Rc8; 8.Bd7 wins) 6.Bd3 Rad8; 7.h5.

(b) "Another common type of blunder is to switch the moves of a planned sequence. After calculating a few moves ahead, you check your analysis to make sure you aren't overlooking something. Then you make the second move of the series instead of the first," wrote Benko, who intended 1...Bxb2+! forcing a draw after 2.Kxb2 Qb4+; 3.Kc1 Qa3+; 4.Kd2 Qa5+!; 5.Kc1 (not 5.c3? Qxa2+) 5...Qa3+ etc.

"This is just about the most heartbreaking kind of blunder," concluded Benko. "You've got a good position, your analysis is correct, your opponent has no idea what's coming — and in a single careless moment you blow it."

SWINDLE OF THE CENTURY

Complacency is just as dangerous as impatience. Reshevsky, a piece ahead with virtually a forced mate in the offing, wondered why I didn't resign. He probably was planning what he was going to have for dinner.

EVANS - RESHEVSKY
USA Championship, 1964

135. Black moves
(a) Qxg3 (b) Qg6

(a) Possibly the most infamous swindle of modern times occurred after 1...Qxg3?; 2.Qg8+! Kxg8; 3.Rxg7+. Only now did Black see that he faced either perpetual check or stalemate. Reshevsky smiled wryly and muttered just one word of reproach to himself: "Stupid!" He shook hands, signed the scoresheet and hurried off without saying another word.

(b) The simplest win is 1...Qg6; 2.Rf8 Qe6; 3.gxf4 Re1+; 4.Kh2 Qa2+; 5.Kh3 Rh1.

PLAN YOUR FOLLOW-UP

Maxims can be confusing. "Always check it may be mate" is contradicted by another maxim, "Nobody ever died from a check." Before deciding if a check is revelant, plan what your next move will be after he gets out of check.

WINTER - CAPABLANCA
Nottingham, 1936

136. White moves
(a) Qh7+ (b) Qc4

(a) Black is threatening mate-in-two by ...Qe4+. In order to gain time Winter decided to give check and only then, after the time control, to evaluate the situation. Alas, on 1.Qh7+? Kg4 he resigned in view of 2.h3+ Kxg3; 3.Rg1+ Qxg1+!; 4.Kxg1 Re1 mate. This illustrates "nobody ever died from a check."

(b) White can win with the obvious 1.Qc4! Qxc4; 2.bxc4 Kg4; 3.Rg8! Kh3 (not 3...Nxf5?; 4.Rf4+) 4.Rh8+ Kg4; 5.Kg1! and the pawn is still immune (5...Nxf5; 6.h3+ Kxg3; 7.Rxf5 Re1+; 8 Rf1.

DEFEATISM
A piece down, White didn't see how to save the game. So he just moved with undue despair and awaited his inevitable doom.

MARSHALL - CAPABLANCA
New York, 1909

137. White moves
(a) Qb5 (b) Qe8+

(a) White eventually lost after the lackluster 1.Qb5? Kg6.

(b) Incredibly, White could have won all the marbles with 1.Qe8+! Kg5; 2.f4+ Kf6 (if 2...Kg4; 3.Qe2 mate) 3.Qh8+ any 4.Qxa1. This illustrates "always check it may be mate."

ANY MOVE WINS

Some positions are so strong that it seems any move will win. This kind of overconfidence is dangerous because you can't afford to relax until the point is in your pocket.

MUELLER - KMOCH
Kecskemet, 1927

138. White moves
(a) Bc7   (b) Ba7

(a) White has an easy win with 1.Bc7! Qxc7; 2.b8/Q+ Qxb8; 3.Qxb8+.

(b) Instead White found 1.Ba7?? Qxa7+ (he forgot it was check!) 2.Kh1 Qb8 but his position was so strong that he still managed to draw after 3.Qb6.

NIGHT MOVES

This position was featured in the movie *Night Moves* starring Gene Hackman as a private eye who studies a pocket chess set while on stakeouts. He explains to a girl how someone once missed a brilliant win and must have regretted it every day of his life. In a way he is talking about himself and his own wasted talent.

EMMRICH - MORITZ
Hamburg, 1922

139. Black moves
(a) Bd5 (b) Qxh2+

(a) Worried about the double attack on his knight at e5, Black panicked with 1...Bd5?; 2.cxd5 Nh3+; 3.Kf1 and then resigned.

(b) The novel *Night Moves* by Alan Sharp identifies the game: "Moritz had had that most flamboyant of possibilities for a chessplayer. Back to the wall, in danger of defeat, he had a queen sacrifice leading to an exquisite mate by means of three little knight moves, prancing in interlocking checks, driving the king into the pit. Moritz, in the heat of something now cold, had missed it, played defensively and lost."

Needless to add, the fantastic missed win is 1...Qxh2+!; 2.Kxh2 Ng4+; 3.Kg1 Nh3+; 4.Kf1 Nh2 mate.

TERROR ON THE LONG DIAGONAL

Ludek Pachman, one of the world's foremost opening theorists, had a momentary lapse in this well-known opening arising from the Queen's Indian Defense. After making his mistake and waiting for his opponent to exploit it, he buttonholed me and said, in broken English: "I'm terrible patzer. See what I overlooked? It's joke. Old 100 years."

JANOSEVICH - PACHMAN
Venice, 1967

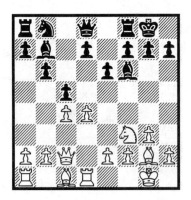

140. Black moves
(a) Nc6 (b) cxd4

(a) After 1...Nc6; 2.dxc5 bxc5 it's a hard game with chances for both sides.

(b) Pachman was familiar with this old trap but forgot about it for the nonce. He played too fast and dropped the exchange after 1...cxd4?; 2.Ng5! Bxg5; 3.Bxb7 Bxc1; 4.Bxa8 Bg5; 5.Rxd4. The rest was a matter of technique.

PERSISTENCE OF VISION

A weird bit of chess history was made when a grandmaster resigned in a winning position after his grandmaster opponent made an error. A rare optical illusion struck them both at the same time.

DARGA - LENGYEL
Amsterdam, 1964

141. Black moves
(a) Bxh4+ (b) R7xe2+

(a) The position is so simplified that a draw is likely after 1...Bxh4+; 2.Ng3 followed by Kg2 breaking the pin.

(b) The time scramble was over and both sides had just passed the control at move 40 but Black, still caught up in the heat of battle, hurriedly played 1...R7xe2+?!? All White had to do was recapture 2.Rxe2 Bxh4+; 3.Ke3! remaining an exchange ahead. But they both overlooked this resource. Darga thought that 3.Kg2? Rxe2+ was forced and extended his hand in the customary gesture of resignation. A moment later he struck his forehead and exclaimed: "My God, I have a winning position!" But it was too late. He had already conceded.

Both players believed the rook on e7 still controlled e3 even after it was gone. A curious case of persistence of vision.

MIDNIGHT OIL

Adjournments are virtually a thing of the past thanks to faster time limits enabling games to finish in a single session. But players used to spend a lot of time burning the midnight oil.

FISCHER - RESHEVSKY
8th match game, 1961

142. White moves
(a) Rc7+ (b) Be4

(a) Fischer told me he reached this position in his home analysis and decided that 1.Rc7+ Rf7; 2.Rxf7+ Kxf7; 3.Bb5! leads to an easy win because Black, in effect, is a piece down and the extra pawn is decisive in the king and pawn ending.

(b) Fischer simply forgot his analysis and played 1.Be4? on the spur of the moment. After 1...Rf7; 2.Bd5 Rd7; 3.Bf3 Rf7; 4.Bh5 Ra7; 5.Rg4+ Kh8; 6.Re4 Kg7; 7.Re6 Na6 the knight came back into play and the extra pawn proved insufficient for victory. Draw.

FIVE PAWNS UP
It's a mystery why White didn't resign long ago. Black is five pawns up and virtually any move wins — except the one he found.

CONGDON - DELMAR
New York, 1880

143. Black moves
(a) Qa1+ (b) Qc3

(a) The simplest path to victory is 1.Qa1+ Kd2; 2.Qb2+.

(b) Instead Black permitted a miraculous draw with 1...Qc3??; 2.Qg8+ Kxg8 stalemate!

GREMLINS STRIKE AGAIN

It's hard to explain why grandmasters sometimes overlook simple mates in the absence of time pressure. The only explanation I can offer is that in the heat of battle they become so intent on their own schemes that they don't consider the opponent's reply. Sound familiar?

STAHLBERG - AVERBACH
Beverwijk, 1963

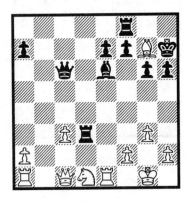

144. Black moves
(a) Kxg7 (b) Bh3

(a) The obvious recapture 1...Kxg7 gives Black a great game. He controls the d-file, has the better pawn structure and also threatens to exploit the weak light squares with Bh3. What more could anyone ask?

(b) Instead Averbach made the worst mistake of his career with 1...Bh3? threatening mate. He was probably busy calculating 2.Ne3 Rxe3 when Stahlberg executed him with 2.Qxh6+ Kg8; 3.Qh8 mate.

WRONG ASSUMPTIONS

White is a queen ahead and needs the pawn on f2 in order to win. Yet it was precisely the presence of this pawn that gulled him into permitting a draw!

YATES - MARSHALL
Carlsbad, 1929

145. White moves
(a) Qc2 (b) Kc4

(a) The correct winning method is 1.Qc2! a3; 2.Kc3 Ka1; 3.Kb3 b1/Q+; 4.Qxb1+ Kxb1; 5.Kxa3 Kc2; 6.f4 and this pawn can't be kept from queening.

(b) Instead White thought he could achieve the same goal by 1.Kc4? b1/Q; 2.Qxb1+ Kxb1; 3.Kb4 but overlooked that 3...Kb2!; 4.Kxa4 Kc3; 5.f4 Kd4; 6.f5 Ke5 draws by catching the pawn. Another famous Marshall "swindle."

FLEETING GLORY

In his first international tournament Arthur Dake, a brash sailor from Oregon, had the mighty Capablanca tied up in knots. Thereby hangs a tail.

CAPABLANCA - DAKE
New York, 1931

146. Black moves
(a) Kxe2   (b) b5

(a) Material is even but Black's outside passed pawn is decisive. Dake wrote: "Capablanca said he would have resigned if I had played the right line. But I did not play wisely and conducted my game in rapid transit style, trying to show the great Capablanca I could play the game as fast as he could."

There was no hurry to take the worthless pawn by 1...Kxe2?; 2.Bxe4 Be8; 2.Bf5 Kf3; 3.e4 Kf4; 4.e5 b5; 5.e6 Bc6? (throws away even the draw which was easy to see by 5...b4; 6.Kc4 Ke5; 7.Kxb4 Kd6) 6.Bg6 b4; 7.Kc5 Ba4; 8.Kxb4 Bc6; 9.Kc5 Ba4; 10.Bh5 Ke3; 11.e7. Black resigns.

(b) Dake observed: "Although the game could have been adjourned, I made the mistake of insisting we finish what we had started." After missing an easy win earlier, he now overlooked another chance to score a full point with 1...b5!; 2.Kc5 Ba8; 3.Kxb5 Kxe2; 4.Kc5 Kxe3 safely harvesting White's pawns.

Chapter 8

PAWN SNATCHING

"The older I grow, the more I value pawns." – Paul Keres

As a charter member of Pawn Snatcher's Anonymous, I can attest that it's worth a good deal of trouble to snatch a lowly pawn. Take it and run unless you see a good reason not to.

But bear in mind Dr. Tarrasch's famous admonition: "Before the endgame the gods have placed the middle game." This means it's not worth jeopardizing your king to amass material because you may never reach old age to enjoy the fruits of your labor.

But in general, let your play be guided by the principle that it's better to be a pawn up than a pawn down. When all other things are equal, an extra pawn rules.

A SAFE SNATCH

"There are no quick knockouts in my games. I like to win a pawn and then 40 moves later win the game," said a postal master. Actually this philosophy applies to over-the-board chess as well.

EVANS - DURAO
Portugal, 1974

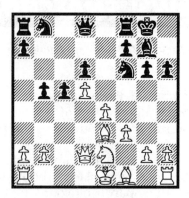

147. White moves
(a) Bxh6 (b) Ng3

(a) The misbegotten 1.Bxh6? Nxe4!; 2.fxe4 Qh4+; 3.g3 Qxh6 lets Black regain the pawn advantageously.

(b) Black must lose a pawn after 1 Ng3! unleashing the dual threat of Bxh6 or Bxb5. The game continued 1...h5; 2.Bxb5 Qb6; 3.Be2 Nfd7; 4.Rb1 Re8; 5.0-0 and it was just a matter of time before White nursed the extra pawn to victory.

A RISKY SNATCH

Before snatching a pawn, you have to weigh the danger. Some players, including myself and Korchnoi, will accept almost any kind of sacrifice. This policy is risky, sometimes foolhardy, and requires supreme faith in your defensive ability.

EVANS - LARSEN
Dallas, 1957

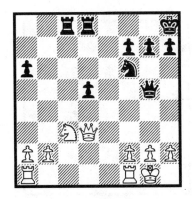

148. White moves
(a) Rad1 (b) Qxa6

(a) A safe way to secure a positional advantage is 1.Rad1 Rc6; 2.Rfe1 — undoubtedly the most prudent path.

(b) Instead I grabbed the pawn by 1.Qxa6!? because it's now or never. But I paid a heavy price after 1...d4; 2.Ne2 Rc2; 3.Rad1 Qe5; 4.Ng3 (I saw too late that 4.Nxd4 Rxd4; 5.Qa8+ Ng8 isn't playable) 4...h5; 5.Rfe1 Qd5; 6.Re2?! d3; 7.Re3 Rxf2! and wins (8.Kxf2 Ng4+).

GOBBLING THE BAIT

Despite having an extra pawn in my pocket, I was unable to find a win in this opposite colored bishop ending. I continued playing out the adjournment because there was still one small trick left.

EVANS - COBO
Havana, 1964

149. Black moves
(a) Rd4 (b) Rxa4

(a) I was prepared to offer a draw after 1...Rd4! because White can't make progress once the threat of Rd7+ is thwarted. 2.Ra7 Be1 holds everything.

(b) Cobo should have smelled a rat. He gobbled the pawn without much hesitation and it cost him the game after 1...Rxa4?; 2.Rd7+ Ke8; 3.Rd5 Rf4 (this pin is the only way to stop Bg6+; if 3...Bc7; 4.Bd7+ spears the king and rook) 4.Re5+ Kd8; 5.Rc5 Rxf5+; 6.Kxf5, etc.

PAWN FIXATION

Here is another illustration of the danger of fixating on a pawn. White is clearly winning but overlooked a neat tactical point.

PETROSIAN - KORCHNOI
Moscow, 1963

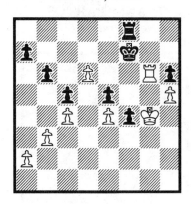

150. White moves
(a) Rxh6 (b) Kf5

(a) "For a long time I had regarded my position as a winning one. Thus the whole opening phase of the struggle, when Korchnoi was unable to get out of trouble, had psychologically attuned me to the idea that the ending would be favorable to me...and here comes the imcomprehensible oversight," writes Petrosian, who gobbled the bait with 1.Rxh6?? (expecting 1...Ke8) and got a rude shock when Korchnoi uncorked 2...f3!! turning the tables.

The concluding moves were 2.Kg5 (if 2.Kxf3 Kg7+ followed by Kxh6 picks up the rook) Ke8! (not 2...f2?; 3.Rf6+ Kg7; 4.Rg6+ Kh7; 5.Rh6+ drawing) and White can't stop the pawn from queening. "If a strong master does not see such a threat at once he will not notice it even if he analyzes the position for 30 minutes" (Petrosian).

(b) It's hard to see how Black can hold out for long after 1.Kf5! If 1...Ke8+; 2.Kxe5 f3; 3.Rg1 f2; 4.Rf1 is decisive.

TAKING THE PLUNGE

Be prepared to face the consequences if you snatch material. Black plunged a knight deep into enemy terrain to win a pawn but now trails in development and must solve the knotty problem of how to extricate the knight.

EVANS - PARTOS
New Jersey, 1950

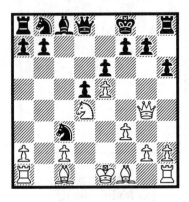

151. Black moves
(a) Nc6 (b) Bd7

(a) After 1...Nc6?; 2.Nxc6 bxc6; 3.Qb4+ Black resigned because he must lose the knight on c3.

(b) The best hope is 1...Bd7 to bring the knight back home via a4. White can regain the pawn by 2.Nxe6+ fxe6; 3.Qb4+ Kf7; 4.Qxc3 Nc6 but it's still a hard game. White keeps the initiative on 1...Qc7; 2.Ba3+ Kg8; 3.Bd6

STORM WARNINGS

It's risky to snatch a pawn when it opens lines that can be used to attack your king. Punishment is often swift and brutal.

EVANS - ZUCKERMAN
USA Championship, 1966

152. Black moves
(a) Nxh5   (b) Qa5

(a) Black thought 1...Nxh5?; 2.Bxg7 Kxg7; 3.g4 Nf6; 4.Qh6+ Kg8 looked safe but he failed to reckon with 5.e5! fxe5; 6.g5 Nh5; 7.Bd3! e4; 8.Rxh5 gxh5; 9.Nxe4! (if 9.Bxe4 Qe5) 9...Qf4; 10.Nf6+ exf6; 11.Bxh7+ Kh8; 12.Bf5+ Kg8; 13.Qh7+ Kf8; 14.Qh8+ Ke7; 15.exf6 mate.

(b) The best defense is 1...Qa5; 2.hxg6 hxg6 (inadequate is 2...Rxc3; 3.Qxc3 Qxa2+; 4.Kc1) and now 3.Bxf6 Bxf6; 4.Nd5 Qxd2; 5.Nxf6+ Kg7!; 6.Nh5+ gxh5; 7.Rxd2 Rh8 may be tenable.

BLINDED BY GREED

White is a pawn up but has to meet the threat of R8d2 doubling rooks. When you're ahead in material, it's more important to consolidate than to swallow more.

PELLETIER - KARPOV
Biel, 1997

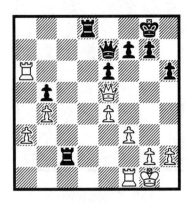

153. White moves
(a) Kh1 (b) Qxb5

(a) After 1.Kh1! Rdd2; 2.Rg1 it's not clear how Black can land a knockout punch. If 2...Qd8; 3.h3 averts immediate disaster.

(b) White lost quickly after the greedy 1.Qxb5? Rdd2; 2.Qb8+ Kh7; 3.Qg3 Qd7 (also good is 3...Qg5) 4.Ra5 Qd4+; 5.Kh1 Rd1. White resigns because his back rank is overpowered.

A TAINTED PAWN

Some players are blinded by material gain. Greed isn't always bad, but it must be tempered with caution.

KREJCIK - AMATEUR
Austria, 1932

154. Black moves
(a) Ra7 (b) Qxb2

(a) The prudent 1...Ra7! guards the second rank and also lends additional support to the pawn on g7.

(b) Black abandoned a beautiful post for his queen and met with disaster by grabbing a tainted pawn: 1...Qxb2?; 2.Qh3+ Kg8; 3.Ne7+ Kf7; 4.Rxg7+! Ke8 (or 4...Kxg7; 5.Nf5+ mates) 5.Qh5+ Kd7; 6.Nc6+ Kxc6; 7.Qd5+ Kb5; 8.Rb7+ Ka4; 9.Qb3+ Qxb3; 10.axb3 mate.

FATAL DISTRACTION

Black's passed pawn should be sufficient for victory. But he gets distracted by the threat to capture his knight.

VAN NUESS - EUWE
Gladbeck, 1928

155. Black moves
(a) Qxh5 (b) Re8

(a) Future world champ Max Euwe chose the natural 1...Qxh5? but was stung by 2.Rxd2! He saw too late that 2...Rxd2?; 3.Qa8 mates. Flustered, he made another error with 2...Re8? (better is 2...Qg5) 3.Qxe8+! Kxe8; 4.Ng7+ followed by Nxh5 snagging a rook.

(b) Black missed a clear win by 1...Re8!; 2.Qf3 Ne5; 3.Qa3+ Kg8; 4.Nd6 Nxc4!; 5.Nxc4 Re1+.

CONSOLIDATE
When ahead in material, your main task is to consolidate. It's more important to batten down the hatches than to go after more booty.

KAN - BOTVINNIK
Moscow, 1935

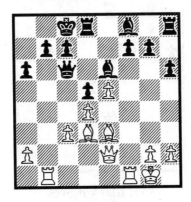

156. Black moves
(a) Qxc3 (b) Be7

(a) Future world champion Botvinnik couldn't resist the urge to grab another pawn even though he already is a pawn up. This injudicious decision merely opened lines for White's attack after 1...Qxc3?; 2.Rfc1 Qa5; 3.Qc2 c6; 4.Bd2 Qc7; 5.Qa4 Rd7; 6.Bxa6 and Black resigns.

(b) White shouldn't get enough compensation for the pawn against careful defense. 1...Be7 mobilizes the bishop and connects rooks on the back rank.

MY KINGDOM FOR A PAWN
The prime directive is to make sure your king is safe. Nothing else really matters if you get mated.

JANSA - GROSS
Pardubice, 1997

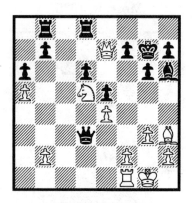

157. Black moves
(a) Qxe4 (b) Kh8

(a) An exchange and pawn ahead, Black blew it with the careless 1...Qxe4?; 2.Qf6+ Kg8; 3.Ne7+ Kf8; 4.Be6 threatening Qxf7 mate.

(b) Black can beat back the attack by 1...Kh8!; 2.Qxf7 Rf8 with every expectation of scoring a full point.

GETTING EVEN

The urge not to fall behind in material can lead you astray. Look what happened to the mighty Capablanca!

CAPABLANCA - FINE
AVRO, 1938

158. White moves
(a) Rxg5 (b) h5

(a) A pawn behind, Capablanca felt constrainted to get it back via the automatic recapture 1.Rxg5? Rb8; 2.Kh3 e5; 3.Rg1 Kf5 and they agreed to a draw.

(b) The passed pawn is decisive after 1.h5! Rb1; 2.Kg2. This resource is so easy to miss that it wasn't even pointed out many years later in a tournament book by Arthur Antler (published in 1993 by Chess Digest).

THE BLOCKADE

White is two pawns down but maintains an effective blockade which ought to be enough to draw. The rook on the sixth rank forbids the Black king from entering the fray.

GUFELD - GULKO
USSR, 1985

159. White moves
(a) Kg3 (b) Kxh5

(a) After 1.Kg3 it's hard for Black to make progress.

(b) Instead White saw a way to win both pawns but failed to reckon with a kicker at the tail end: 1.Kxh5? g3; 2.Ra1 g2; 3.Rg1 Kf6; 4.Kh4 Kf5; 5.Kh3 Kf4; 6.Kh2 (if 6.Rxg2 Rh7 mate) 6...Kf3; 7.Rf1+ gxf1/B and White resigned.

DISASTER AFTER ADJOURNMENT

Bobby Fischer's games are largely error-free. This blunder is all the more remarkable because it took place immediately after the game was resumed and White's sealed move (Na7c8) was revealed on the board.

ELISKASES - FISCHER
Buenos Aires, 1960

160. Black moves
(a) Bxa3 (b) Bc5

(a) Black has an easy draw by 1...Bxa3!; 2.Nxb6 Bxb2; 3.Nxc4 Bc1; 4.f5 h5 and White's extra pawn is meaningless.

(b) Failing to snatch a pawn at the right moment can be just as bad as taking one at the wrong moment. Perhaps Fischer hoped to trap the knight by 1...Bc5? but he overlooked 2.a4! (instead of 2.Na7 Bd4) leaving him a pawn down without compensation. White won after 2...Kg6; 3.Kg2 Kf6; 4.Kf3 Ke6; 5.Ke4 Bf2; 6.f5+ Kd7; 7.Na7 Kd6; 8.Nb5+ Kc5; 9.Nc7 Bh4; 10.Ne8 Kb4; 11.Kd5 Be7; 12.Nxg7 Bf6; 13.Ne8 Bxb2; 14.f6 Bxf6; 15.Nxf6 c3; 16.Nh5! Kxa4 (or 16...c2; 17.Nf4 Kc3; 18.Ne2+ Kd2; 19.Nd4 c1/Q; 20.Nb3+ and Nxc1) 17.Nf4 c2; 18.Ne2. Black resigned.

HIT AND RUN

White is a piece down. He can either recapture it immediately or take a detour by seizing a pawn deep in enemy territory.

HAAS - WOLF
Vienna, 1912

161. White moves
(a) fxe3 (b) Qxg7

(a) White had aimed for this position and rejected 1.fxe3 0-0 because of his horrible pawn structure and lack of development, but it was now the only hope to prolong the game.

(b) Instead White carried out his plan to snatch a pawn by 1.Qxg7? (hoping to hit and run after 1...Rf8; 2.fxe3) but fell victim to 1...Qg5!; 2.Qxh8+ Ke7; 3.Qxh7 Bxf2+!; 4.Kh1 (a smothered mate ensues on 4.Rxf2 Qc1+; 5.Rf1 Qe3+; 6.Kh1 Nf2+; 7.Kg1 Nh3+; 8.Kh1 Qg1+!; 9.Rxg1 Nf2) 4...Rg8; 5.Qh3 Bc8; 6.Qf3 Ng3+! White resigned since 7.hxg3 Rh8 mates or 7.Qxg3 Bxg3 costs the queen.

LOOK BOTH WAYS

White's knight is threatened. Is there any reason why it can't snatch a pawn, or must it retreat?

MILTON - LUGOWOI
Russia, 1998

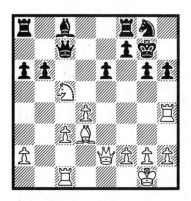

162. White moves
(a) Nxa6 (b) Nb3

(a) White's pieces are so far-flung that he should suspect some sort of retaliation for 1.Nxa6? Bxa6; 2.Bxa6 even though it seems like a safe pawn snatch. But he forgot to look at both sides of the board or he might have seen 2...Qe7!; 3.Rf4 Qa3! This unusual maneuver gains a piece after 4.Rb1 Rxa6; 5.Qe5+ Kh7; 6.Qc7 Qe7 and White resigns.

(b) Since White really doesn't have serious attacking chances with his misplaced rook on h4, he should retreat 1.Nb3 to lend more support to the pawn on d4 after 1...Bb7; 2.c4.

TEMPTING FATE
This is one of the most dramatic moments in chess history. After endless machinations, America's Bobby Fischer finally arrived in Iceland for a Cold War showdown with Russia's Boris Spassky. At the outset Fischer tried too hard to win a drawn ending.

SPASSKY - FISCHER
1st match game, 1972

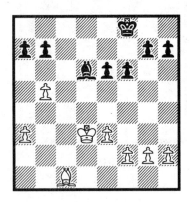

163. Black moves
(a) Ke7 (b) Bxh2

(a) Neither side can make progress after 1...Ke7.

(b) After due deliberation, instead of acquiescing to a draw, Fischer tried to win with 1...Bxh2?! and Spassky bolted upright in his chair. Play continued 2.g3 h5; 3.Ke2 h4; 4.Kf3. "Fischer must see something we don't," whispered a reverential fan (when it became obvious that 4...h3; 5.Kg4 Bg1; 6.Kxh3 Bxf2; 7.Bd2! traps the bishop). So Black had to settle for 4...Ke7; 5.Kg2 hxg3; 6.fxg3 Bxg3; 7.Kxg3 Kd6; 8.a4 Kd5; 9.Ba3 Ke4; 10.Bc5 a6; 11.b6! f5; 12.Kh4 f4? (the last chance to draw was 12...Kd5) 13.exf4 Kxf4; 14.Kh5 and Spassky went on to win.

Snatching the pawn was strategically wrong because it gave Fischer losing chances without any winning prospects. The best he could hope for was a draw which was his for the asking at the outset.

MAKING THE BEST OF IT
White's position is clearly inferior because of his weakened pawn structure. But it went from bad to hopeless when he failed to make the most of his chances.

SHIROV - ANAND
Linares, 1998

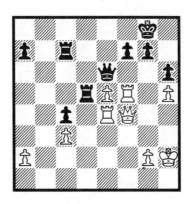

164. White moves
(a) Rxc4 (b) Re1

(a) White walked into a lost ending after 1.Rxc4? Qxf5! (perhaps he was hoping for 1...Rxc4; 2.Qxc4 Qxf5; 3.Qxd5 Qxh5+; 4.Kg1) 2.Qxf5 Rxc4; 3.Qb1 Rd8; 4.Qb7 Rxc3; 5.Qxa7 Rcc8 and the rest was a matter of technique. For the record, the conclusion was: 6.a4 Ra8; 7.Qc7 Rdc8; 8.Qb7 Re8; 9.Qc7 Rac8; 10.Qd7 Rcd8; 11.Qc7 Rd5; 12.a5 Rdxe5.

(b) The best hope is to stand pat with 1.Re1. If 1...Rd3; 2.Rb1 offers counterplay (2...Rxc3; 3.Rb8+ Kh7; 4.Qe4). Or 1...Rcc5; 2.Rf1 Rxe5; 3.Rxf7 Rxh5+; 4.Kg1 giving up a pawn for control of the 7th rank.

DON'T BE A PATSY

White just took a pawn on e5 with his knight, exposing his queen to capture. Would you believe that it was all over in just three more moves?

BERGER - FROHLICH
Graz, 1888

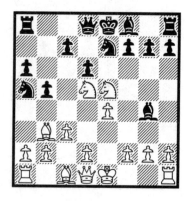

165. Black moves
(a) Bxd1 (b) dxe5

(a) Taken by surprise, Black gobbled the bait with 1...Bxd1?; 2.Nf6+! gxf6; 3.Bxf7 mate. This ancient trap involving mate on f7 has surfaced in many guises through the ages.

(b) Simply 1...dxe5! (better than 1...Nxb3; 2.Nxg4 Nxa1?; 3.Nf6+ gxf6; 4.Nxf6 mate) 2.Qxg4 Nxb3; 3.axb3 Nxd5; 4.exd5 Qxd5; 5.b4 leads to even chances.

SCORPION STING
White can either win a pawn or threaten to win a pawn. Which plan is better and why?

AROND - DELAY
Chicago, 1997

166. White moves
(a) Bxh7+ (b) Ng5

(a) White thought he could win a pawn but missed a scorpion sting at the tail end of his combination after 1.Bxh7+? Kxh7; 2.Qd3+ Kg8; 3.Qxd7 Rad8; 4.Qa4 Qc6; 5.Qc2 Qe4; 6.Qb3 (of no avail is 6.Qxe4 Rxd1+; 7.Qe1 Bxf3) 6...c4; 7.Qa4 Bc6 and now White must either lose his overburdened queen or get mated on the back rank.

(b) If White had seen ahead a little further, he might have chosen 1 Ng5 stepping up the pressure against h7.

AVOID CREATING HOLES

Pawns should be advanced with care since they are the only unit that can never retreat. Here White has a choice between two pawn moves, but one needlessly creates a glaring weakness.

FRANK - EVANS
USA Open, 1948

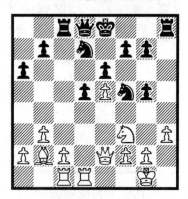

167. White moves
(a) c4 (b) g4

(a) White has a very good game and can increase his advantage by 1.c4! striking at the center. Indeed, it's not clear if Black can survive after 1...dxc4; 2.Rxc4.

(b) To my great surprise White created a self-inflicted hole on f4 by 1.g4? Nh4; 2.Nxh4 Rxh4; 3.Kg2? (better is 3.Qe3) 3...Nf8!; 4.Ra1 Ng6; 5.Bc1 Rc3 (invading on another hole) 6.Rd3 Qc7 and suddenly Black's pieces have all sprung to life.

Chapter 9

CREATING WEAKNESSES

"The pawn is the soul of chess." – Philidor

The pawn is unique. All other chessmen can go either backwards or forwards at will, but the foot soldier may never retreat. When you push a pawn early on, try to make sure you won't regret it on the day of reckoning. Weaknesses are the result of damage to the pawn structure, such as holes which can't be repaired.

The three elements of chess – space, time and force – constantly change after each move. But pawn structure is enduring.

INNOCUOUS PAWN PUSHES

Every time you move it strengthens one square and weakens another. Since pieces can retreat, wrongs often can be rectified. But pawns are there to stay.

STEVENS - EVANS
New York, 1946

168. White moves
(a) 0-0 (b) a3

(a) Since White has nothing better to do he should castle and await further developments. Also feasible is 1.d5.

(b) The innocuous 1.a3? creates a target on b3, loses time, and proved disastrous after 1...Na5! winning at least a pawn owing to the threat of Nb3. If 2.c5 Nb3; 3.Qd1 Nxa1; 4.cxb6 Nc2+ extricates the knight.

UNGUARDED SQUARES

Material is even and White doesn't seem to be in any immediate danger. But Satan never sleeps!

SIEMMS - EVANS
USA Junior Championship, 1949

169. White moves
(a) Bd4 (b) Nb3

(a) White lost in a jiffy by relinquishing the guard over f4 by 1.Bd4? Nf4; 2.Qg3 (or 2.Qf1 c5; 3.Be3 Bd3) 2...Ne2 mate. Another mistake would be 1.c4? Nb4.

(b) A reasonable defense to the threat of Qa5 is 1.Nb3. Also feasible is 1.Nc4. In any case it still would be a hard game.

PLUGGING LEAKS

Black has a hole on c6 because the pawns which normally guard that square have already advanced. He should try to plug the leak without calling in the plumbers.

EVANS - JOYNER
USA Junior Championship, 1949

170. Black moves
(a) Nd7 (b) c6

(a) 1...Nd7? led to disaster because 2.Nc6! occupied the hole and won a pawn after 2...Qf6; 3.Bxd6 Qxd6; 4.Bxd5! Rfe8 (the bishop is invulnerable since 5.Qxd5? Ne7+ forks the queen) 5.Bf3 Nf6; 6.Rfc1 Nd5; 7.Qc4 etc.

(b) Black stands worse but might be able to plug the leak with 1...c6 to avert immediate material loss.

STANDING PAT

Most players can't stand passive positions, and who can blame them? But sometimes there is nothing to do but stand pat.

EVANS - MCCORMICK
Lone Pine, 1971

171. White moves
(a) c5 (b) Kd3

(a) White is clearly worse because my king can't stray too far from the kingside where it must keep an eye on the protected passed pawn. But I got impatient and virtually forced Black to find the win!

The game continued 1.c5? Ka6; 2.Kd4 Kb7; 3.Ke4 Kc6; 4.Kd4 Kb5!; 5.Kd5 g3; 6.c6 Kb6!; 7.Kd6 g2; 8.c7 g1/Q; 9.c8/Q Qd4+; 10.Ke7 Qxh4+; 11.Kf8 Qf4+; 12.Ke8 (or 12.Kg8 Qg4+; 13.Qxg4 hxg4 wins) 12...Qe5+ and I resigned since there's no way to prevent a queen swap after 13.Kf7 Qc7+ or 13.Kd8 Qh8+.

(b) Instead of rashly advancing the pawn, White must stand pat. The best chance to draw is 1.Kd3! Ka4; 2.Ke4 (2.c5? Kb5; 3.Kd4 Kc6 puts White in zugzwang) 2...Kb4; 3.Kd4! (but not 3.Kd3? Kc5!; 4.Kc3 g3 wins) and Black can't make headway.

SELF-INFLICTED WOUNDS

Pawns can be used as battering rams to weaken enemy outposts. But aggression must be tempered with caution.

LIEBERT - EVANS
Siegen Olympiad, 1970

172. Black moves
(a) h4   (b) Bg7

(a) I had visions of opening the h-file to attack with 1...h4? but this brainstorm proved defective after 2.g4 h3?! (it's too late to turn back with 2...Ne7; 3.f4 Bg7; 4.Bxh4) 3.gxf5 exf5; 4.f4! (the fly in the ointment) 4...Bg7; 5.Ng5 Re8; 6.Nxh3 Rxe3; 7.Qg2 and White's extra piece ultimately prevailed.

(b) I pressed too hard to create an imbalance. The prudent 1...Bg7 maintains equality.

DOING NOTHING

Black stands worse and shouldn't try to get fancy. It's hard to sit back and wait, but sometimes you just have to hang on and do nothing.

EVANS - KARKLINS
Lone Pine, 1972

173. Black moves
(a) Rf8 (b) h4

(a) Black would like to play 1...Ng5 but sees that 2.Rg3 h4; 3.Rxg5! Qxg5; 4.Qxf7 wins a piece. Correct is 1...Rf8! (with the threat of Ng5) and it's hard to see how White can make progress.

(b) Black created an egregious weakness with 1...h4? hoping for 2.Qd8? Ng5; 3.Rf1 Nxh3+. But it ended fast after 2.Rf4 Qh5?; 3.Rxe4!

WEAKENED FORTRESS

Sometimes it's necessary to push a pawn whether you like it or not. But be wary of advancing too many pawns in front of your castled king.

STEIN - EVANS
Amsterdam, 1964

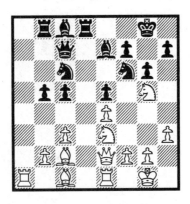

174. Black moves
(a) h6 (b) c4

(a) Black's fortress looks secure after 1...h6; 2.Nf3 Be6. However the refutation of 1...h6? came swiftly via 2.Nd5! Nxd5; 3.exd5 hxg5 (if 3...Rxd5; 4.Qf3!) 4.dxc6 Qxc6; 5.Qxe5 Bb7; 6.Qg3 Qf6; 7.Rxe7! Qxe7; 8.Bxg5 f6; 9.Bf4 Ra8; 10.Rxa8 Bxa8; 11.Bxg6 Qg7; 12.Be3 c4; 13.Bf7+! Kxf7; 14.Qc7+ Kg6; 15.Qxd8 Bc6; 16.Bd4 Qf7; 17.Qd6 and Black resigns.

(b) The only decent move at Black's disposal is 1...c4 to get some elbow room. If 2.b3 (not 2.Qf3? h6; 3.Nd5 Qd6! snares a piece; or 2.Nd5 Nxd5; 3.exd5 Bxg5; 4.Bxg5 Rxd5) 2...Na5 offering just enough counterplay to hold the balance.

COMEDY OF ERRORS

Black wants to castle but must first prevent Bxh7+. Some weakening of the kingside is unavoidable no matter which pawn he pushes.

SZABO - RESHEVSKY
Zurich, 1953

175. Black moves
(a) h6 (b) g6

(a) The lesser evil is 1...h6 and the game probably would continue normally after 2.0-0 0-0.

(b) Reshevsky chose 1...g6 weakening a cluster of dark squares on the kingside which showed up later after 2.h4! h5; 3.Rb1 Rb8; 4.Be4 Qc7; 5.0-0 Bd7; 6.d5 exd5; 7.Bxd5 Bf6; 8.Ng5 Nd8 (if 8...Bxg5; 9.hxg5 Qe5; 10.e4) 9.c4 Bc6; 10.Ne4 Bg7; 11.Bb2 0-0; 12.Nf6+. (See next diagram.)

DOUBLE TROUBLE

Black's position is now hopeless. But gremlins plagued both players.

SZABO - RESHEVSKY
Zurich 1953

176. Black moves
(a) Kh8 (b) Bxf6

(a) The only way to avert disaster is 1...Kh8. In the tournament book David Bronstein notes: "White would have continued his attack by 2.f4 followed by f5 or e4-e5 with a relatively easy win. Those with a penchant for beauty might try 2.Qc3 threatening Ne8 and 2...Bxd5 would be well met by 3.Nxd5."

(b) One of the most amazing double blunders in the annals of chess occurred after 1...Bxf6? when Szabo missed 2.Qxg6+ Bg7; 3.Qxg7 mate. Later, when explaining this extraordinary gaffe, he said: "Well, you don't just look for mates in two against Reshevsky."

After 2.Bxf6?? Szabo's position was still overwhelming. The comedy of errors continued: 2...Bxd5; 3.cxd5 Qd6; 4.Qc3 Qxd5; 5.Rfd1 Qf5; 6.e4 Qe6; 7.Bg7 b6. (See next diagram.)

A FINAL TWIST

After so many missed opportunities, White still had a chance to make amends. But he botched it once again.

SZABO - RESHEVSKY
Zurich 1953

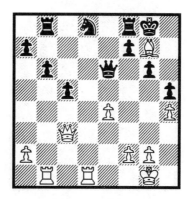

177. White moves
(a) Bh6 (b) Bxf8

(a) Turning once more to Bronstein's notes: "White's position is so powerful that despite his unbelievable blunder earlier he still has more than enough to win. Once again, it comes down to a mate threat at g7, for which purpose he need only have retreated his bishop by 1.Bh6 forcing 1...f6 when 2.Qg3 (with the double threat of Qxg6 or Qxb8) would have won at least a rook."

(b) After 1.Bxf8? Kxf8 Bronstein writes: "Szabo immediately saw his error and became so distraught that after using up nearly all his remaining time, and still without making a move, he accepted the draw Reshevsky had offered nearly half an hour before. After such a traumatic experience Szabo was a long time regaining his confidence, which naturally affected his play for the remainder of the tournament." In George Bernard Shaw's memorable phrase, he played the rest of his games like a squashed cabbage leaf.

COMMITTING SUICIDE

Opening lines that prove helpful to the enemy is a special form of suicide. Especially when your own king is the target.

EVANS - YANOFSKY
Dallas, 1957

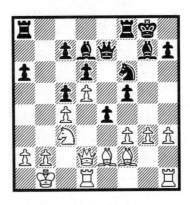

178. White moves
(a) fxe4 (b) f4

(a) After 1.fxe4? Nxe4; 2.Nxe4 fxe4; 3.Be3 Rab8. I was curiously helpless against the combined onslaught of bishop and rook on b2. On 4.b3 Qe5 I resigned.

(b) I should have kept the lines closed with 1.f4 Rab8; 2.Be3 Rb7; 3.Rc1 Rfb8; 4.Rc2 lending support to the weak point on b2. Even 1 g4 is better than what I played.

PROPHYLAXIS

Prophylaxis is Nimzovich's wonderful term for restraining your opponent from expanding or freeing his game. It often involves making a move that seems to have little bearing on the action.

SHIRLEY - EVANS
San Diego Open, 1955

179. White moves
(a) h3 (b) f4

(a) The best move is 1.h3! to deny the knight access to g4. Now White is ready for f4. There is nothing to fear from 1...Bxh3?; 2.Bxh3 Nf3+; 3.Kg2 Nxe1+; 4.Rxe1 gaining two pieces for a rook.

(b) Instead White prematurely kicked the knight by 1.f4? Ng4 and his position soon fell apart after 2.Bd2? (also awkward is 2.Bf2 Bf8!) 2...Bd4+; 3.Kf1 Rxc5; 4.Qa4 Nxh2+; 5.Ke2 Bg4+; 6.Kd3 Bb2 and White resigned.

BACKWARD PAWNS

A backward pawn can no longer be defended by pawns of the same color behind it. Sometimes it's necessary to create this weakness to obtain freedom for your pieces, but be wary if the pawn can later become a target along an open file.

DURAS - CHAJES
Carlsbad,1911

180. Black moves
(a) f5 (b) h6

(a) Black's position already is unpleasant because White controls more space yet 1...f5? made matters worse by saddling him with a serious weakness — a backward pawn on an open file at e6 that led to his downfall. He kicked the bishop back for one move, 2.Bc2, and then spent the rest of the game nursing his wound. Black would be okay if he could dissolve the target with 2...e5 but this would be refuted by 2.Ng5! Qf6; 3.c5 Be7; 4.Qh5. The game continued 2...Nf6; 3.Qe2 b6; 4.b3 a5; 5.Bb2 Qc7; 6.Rad1 Re8; 7.Rfe1 dominating the central files while Black had to sit back and suffer.

(b)Black would like to free his game by 1...e5 but this costs a pawn after 2.dxe5 Nxe5; 3.Nxe5 Bxe5; 4.Bxh7+ (better than 4.Qh5 f5) 4...Kxh7; 5.Qh5+ Kg8; 6.Qxe5. The lesser evil is 1...h6; 2.Re1 Nf6; 3.Bc2 b6 slowly trying to work his way out of the cramp.

DOUBLED PAWNS

Doubled pawns create a semi-open file to work on, but as a rule they should be avoided. Here White has an isolated pawn on d4 and must meet the threat of Bxf3 ripping open his kingside.

SANDRIN - EVANS
USA Open, 1951

181. White moves
(a) Be2 (b) Rc5

(a) The retreat 1.Be2 props up the knight and also defends the pawn on d4.

(b) White inexplicably ignored his pawn structure and lost after 1.Rc5? Bxf3; 2.gxf3 Rad8; 3.Rb5 Qc6; 4.Rc1 Qd7; 5.Bc4 Nb6; 6.b3 Bxd4.

REPAIRING WEAKNESSES

It bears repeating that since the pawn is the only unit that can never retreat, it should be advanced with caution. My pawn on e4 is isolated and therefore weak because no pawn behind it can come to its aid at either d3 or f3.

EVANS - POSCHEL
USA Championship, 1948

182. White moves
(a) Na5 (b) e5

(a) 1.Na5 contains a cheap threat that can be foiled easily by either 1...b6 or c5. It ignores the long-range problem of a weak pawn on e4.

(b) This is a case where, as so very often happens, tactics supplement strategy. I was trying to find a way to eliminate my laggard pawn and tactics presented the proper moment to do so with 1.e5! based on the momentary pin of the d-pawn. Taken aback, my opponent blundered by 1...Nxe5? (relatively best is 1...Rd8) 2.Nxe5 Bxe5; 3.Rxf8+ Qxf8; 4.Bxe5 c5; 5.Qf4! and Black resigns.

IN THE LONG RUN
Balancing short term advantages against long term weaknesses
can be vexing. Here White is faced with the critical decision of
how to recapture the knight on d3 — with pawn or knight? Both
moves are tempting.

ALBIN - SCHIFFERS
Nuremberg, 1896

183. White moves
(a) cxd3 (b) Nxd3

(a) Black stands better because he has just captured a strong
bishop on d3. White retook 1.cxd3? which looks good in the
short run because he can occupy the c-file with a rook, retain
the knight on e5, and also prevent an enemy knight from perch-
ing on e4. But in the long run, doubled pawns are a permanent
disability that can't be easily dissolved. After 1...Bd7; 2.g4 Bb5;
3.g5 Nd7; 4.Rc1 Qd8; 5.Ndf3 f6 repulsed the attack and now
Black was able to focus on the weak pawns.

(b) While 1.Nxd3 is not ideal it prevents doubled pawns. After
1...b6; 2.c4 Ba6; 3.Rc1 it's still a hard game.

RELIEVING CRAMPS

White clearly has an advantage in space since Black's bishops are still consigned to the back row. In order to relieve the cramp, Black must drive the knight away from d5. But how?

DJURIC - COLLAS
Corsica, 1997

184. Black moves
(a) e6   (b) Qd8

(a) In his anxiety to relieve the cramp, Black created a hole on f6 by 1...e6? which allowed 2.Bb6! Nxb6; 3.Nf6+ Kh8; 4.Nxe8 Qb4; 5.b3 Nd7; 6.Qb2+ Kg8; 7.a5 and Black resigns.

(b) Since the queen isn't well-placed anyway, the paradoxical retreat 1...Qd8 is the best chance to survive. Black's position is not pleasant, but e6 on the next move will offer some relief by driving the knight back.

FIGHTING AGAINST BINDS

Most players hate positions in which they are reduced to total passivity. But sometimes we must be patient enough to realize when there is nothing to do but sit back and wait.

NAJDORF - OPOCENSKY
Prague, 1946

185. Black moves
(a) Nf6 (b) g5

(a) It's hard to see how White can breakthrough after 1...Nf6 followed by Kg8 and Kg7 forever. For better or worse this is the only defense that offers any chance to draw.

(b) Black figured he neded an active defense to hold the draw and fatally weakened his pawns by 1...g5? which lost to 2.Kh3! Kg8; 3.hxg5 Nxg5+; 4.Kh4 Nh7; 5.Kxh5 Kg7; 6.g4 Nf6+; 7.Kh4 Kg8. Black didn't bother to resume after adjournment in view of 8.g5 Nh7; 9.Ng4 Kg7; 10.Kh5 Rh8; 11.Nh6! Nxg5; 12.Kxg5 Rxh6; 13.Rxf7+ Kxf7; 14.Kxh6.

LETTING YOUR GUARD DOWN

Both sides are barely out of the opening and the position looks fairly even. It's hard to believe that White will lose in just a few more moves.

STAHLBERG - PETROSIAN
Zurich, 1953

186. White moves
(a) Nd3 (b) Bh3

(a) Correct is 1.Nd3 offering to trade a passive piece for Black's active knight.

(b) The pawn on e4 is so well protected that White removed one of its guards by 1.Bh3? and forgot this lost a pawn by 1...Bxh3; 2.Kxh3 Nxe4!; 3.Nxe4 Qf5+; 4.Kh2 Qxe4. The commentators justifiably called it an unbelievable blunder.

THE BETTER PART OF VALOR

There's an old saying that caution is the better part of valor. Don't start anything you're not prepared to finish.

MARCO - MAROCZY
Ostend, 1905

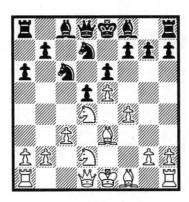

187. Black moves
(a) g5 (b) Be7

(a) In a desire to weaken the pawn chain Black played the ugly 1...g5? (hoping for 2.g3 gxf4; 3.gxf4 Qh4+) but was rocked by 2.Nxe6! fxe6; 3.Qh5+ Ke7; 4.f5 Nf6; 5.Bc5+ and had to resign since 5...Kd7; 6.Qf7+ Be7; 7.fxe6+ Kc7; 8.exf6 is crushing.

(b) Since Black can't relieve his cramp by violent means, he has nothing better than to quietly pursue development with 1...Be7; 2.Bd3 0-0.

FORTIFY WEAK POINTS

White left his king in the center in order to pursue an attack along the h-file. But is Black in any real danger?

MARSHALL - BURN
Paris, 1900

188. Black moves
(a) Nd7 (b) Kg7

(a) The careless developing move 1...Nd7? led to disaster after 2.Bxg6! fxg6; 3.Qxg6+ Bg7; 4.Ng5 Qf6; 5.Rh8+! Kxh8; 6.Qh7 mate.

(b) By simply fortifying g6 with 1...Kg7, Black not only prevents the sacrifice but also neutralizes the open h-file and poses White with the problem of where to find a home for his own king.

Chapter 10

INATTENTION

*"There have been times in my life when I came very near to thinking
that I could not lose even a single game. Then I would be beaten,
and the lost game would bring me back from dreamland to earth."*
— Jose Capablanca

In a sense all errors can be attributed to "inattention." Under this category I have lumped oversights that don't seem to fit neatly elsewhere, such as resigning in a won or drawn position.

Most of these goofs can be ascribed to fatigue and shortage of time rather than lack of skill or experience. After all, they were perpetrated by some of the world's greatest players.

Sit back and enjoy!

PLAYING BY ROTE

The Ruy Lopez is so heavily analyzed that both sides often rattle off a series of book moves that land them in the middle game before they know it. The Breyer Defense has been repeated in countless games: 1.e4 e5; 2.Nf3 Nc6; 3.Bb5 a6; 4.Ba4 Nf6; 5.0-0 Be7; 6.Re1 b5; 7.Bb3 d6; 8.c3 0-0; 9.h3 Nb8; 10.d4 Nbd7; 11.Nbd2.

POLGAR - SPASSKY
10th match game, 1993

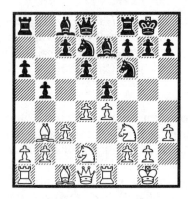

189. Black moves
(a) Re8 (b) Bb7

(a) Ex-world champ Boris Spassky already chose this defense twice in his match against 16-year-old Judith Polgar in Budapest that was dubbed "the battle of the generations." She won 5 1/2 - 4 1/2 despite this amazing incident when he mixed up the order of his moves by 1...Re8? and she missed 2.Bxf7+! Kxf7; 3.Ng5+ Kg8; 4.Ne6 snaring his queen. Instead, barely glancing at the board, she transposed into the main line with 2.Nf1 Bb7.

Indeed, not exploiting a mistake is a mistake. Pal Benko, who was doing live commentary for the audience, noted: "I thought the messenger reported the game wrongly. So I verified with the players, and indeed that double blunder happened. It's funny, but the players were not aware of it."

(b) The correct move order is 1...Bb7 because now 2.Bxf7+? Kxf7; 2.Ng5+ Kg8; 3.Ne6 Qc8 refutes the sacrifice. They both glided through the opening by rote at breakneck speed and finally reached this endgame. Usually it's possible to draw when all the pawns are on the same side of the board, but Polgar thought she was lost and failed to find the best defense.

ROOKS SHOULD RAMPAGE

Rooks really come into their own in the endgame when the board is relatively uncluttered. In order to profit from the open lines, they should seek active rather than passive posts.

POLGAR - SPASSKY
10th match game 1993

190. White moves
(a) Rf3 (b) Rb7

(a) White lost by force after 1.Rf3? f5; 2.Rf4 Re2!; 3.Kh1 Re4; 4.Rf2 Kh4; 5.Kg2 Rb4; 6.Kh2 Re4; 7.Kg2 f4; 8.Kf3 Re5; 9.Rg2 g5; 10.Rg4+ Kxh3; 11.Rg3+ Kh4!

(b)White should maneuver the rook behind enemy lines where it has room to do its job. The drawing line is 1.Rb7! f5; 2.Rg7 g5 (or 2...f4; 3.Rh7+ Kg5; 4.Rf7 Ra4; 5.Kg2) 3.Rh7+ Kg6; 4.Rh8 f4; 5.h4! gxh4 (if 5...g4; 6.Rg8+ Kf5; 7.Rg5+) 6.Rxh4 Kf5; 7.Rh3 Ke4; 8.Rb3 f3; 9.Rb8 with an elementary book draw.

TOUCH MOVE!

As we have seen, sometimes a given move order has been played so often that the players scarcely glance at the board before making a reply. This has happened occasionally in the Petrov Defense after 1.e4 e5; 2.Nf3 Nf6; 3.Nxe5 d6; 4.Nf3 Nxe4; 5.d3.

TARRASCH - ALAPIN
Breslau, 1889

191. Black moves
(a) Nf6 (b) Be7

(a) The knight is attacked and should retreat to f6 from whence it came.

(b) Black hurriedly played 1...Be7? and resigned after 2.dxe4. This weird mistake came about because Alapin had expected the customary d4 instead of d3. Imagine his chagrin when he took another look at the board and saw that his knight was en prise!

GETTING AHEAD OF YOURSELF

Who says there's no luck in chess? I was ready to resign when my opponent presented me with an unexpected gift.

FEUERSTEIN - EVANS
USA Championship, 1971

192. White moves
(a) Rxb6 (b) Rxc4

(a) Black's position is horrible but I can still offer token resistance after 1.Rxb6 e6; 2.Qa4 Qa7; 3.Kh2 d5; 4.Rb7 Qa8.

(b) My opponent squelched all possible counterplay by 1.Rxc4! Nxc4 but instead of following it up with 2.Nb5 when I was prepared to extend my hand, he instantly played 2.Nd5?? which looks just as crushing (since 2...Qxc6; 3.Nxe7+ forks the queen). He overlooked 2...Qa7! indirectly protecting the knight (3.Qxc4? b5+). The game ended quickly in my favor after 3.c7 Rxc7; 4.Nxc7 Qxc7; 5.Kh2 Qc5; 6.Qa4 d5; 7.e4 dxe4; 8.Rb5 Qc6; 9.Qb4 Ra8 and White resigns.

This mistake occurred because White already determined what his next move would be before playing 1.Rxc4! In other words, he played two moves at once rather than one at a time. Surely he would have seen this defensive resource had he spent a few more seconds to check his follow-up instead of playing it without taking another look at the board.

ANOTHER MIRAGE

Turnabout is fair play. I was the victim of a similar mirage and still curse myself whenever I think about it.

EVANS - SHERWIN
USA Championship, 1959

193. White moves
(a) Bf1 (b) Bxc4

(a) After 1.Bf1? I was stunned by 1...Bxe4!; 2.fxe4 Ng4!; 3.g3 Ne3; 4.Qe2 Nxd1; 5.Rxd1 Rxd1; 6.Qxd1 Qxe4; 7.Bc1 h6; 8.a4 Qe1. It was just a matter of time before Black asserted his material advantage.

(b) Later it dawned on me that the bishop is immune after 1.Bxc4! Qc5+; 2.Rd4! interposing the rook. Now on 2...b5 (if 2...Rxd4; 3.cxd4) 3.Bb3 Black has nothing to show for the pawn. Or on 1.Bxc4 Bxe4 White can safely play 2.Qf2 without even worrying about any of the complications arising from 2.fxe4 Ng4.

NEVER SAY DIE!

Nobody ever won by resigning. If there's a trick left, try it. But here Black gave up without bothering to make one more move by sliding his queen from d3 to d4, hoping for a last-minute swindle.

YERMOLINSKY - SALOV
Wijk aan Zee, 1997

194. Black moves
(a) Kh7 (b) Kg8

(a) Robert Byrne in the New York Times pointed out that Black resigned because "1...Kh7! decisively unpins the f6 pawn" threatening f5. Yet he overlooked that 2.Qd7+! Qxd7; 3.Nxf6+ Kg7; 4.Nxd7 gives White good drawing chances.

(b) It's true that Black is lost because of the threat of f5. The right move is 1...Kg8!; 2.Qc4+ Kh7; 3.Qd4 Re7! to stop Qd7 once and for all. Before throwing in the towel, Salov should have waited for his opponent to find a finesse that eluded an annotator in the cold light of day.

WEARING 'EM DOWN

I had a clear advantage but couldn't seem to make headway in a long drawn-out ending where a locked pawn structure made it almost impossible to find any points of entry. A draw seemed likely, but I kept plodding because only Black has winning chances.

BINET-EVANS
USA Open, 1971

195. White moves
(a) Ra1 (b) Nb3

(a) White must bar the king from penetrating to d5 and c4. After 1.Ra1 Bb6; 2.Nb3 Black is stymied and can't make progress.

(b) To my great surprise, after mounting a sturdy defense, White tired and let my king penetrate by 1.Nb3? Kc6; 2.Nd4+ Kd5. Now White's position crumbled after 3.b3 a4; 4.b4 Bb6; 5.Bg1 Rb7; 6.Be3 Ba7; 7.Ra1 Re7; 8.Ra2 Kc4; 9.Rb2 Kd5; 10.Ra2 Rc7; 11.Ra1 Bxd4 (finally); 12.Bxd4 Kc4; 13.Bc5 Rd7; 14.Bd6 Kb3 and the threat of Kb2 followed by Kxa3 is decisive.

Moral: Keep pressing an advantage. Give your opponent a chance to help you.

GIVE 'EM ROPE

World champion Tigran Petrosian was always hard to beat. He seldom took risks, rarely made mistakes, and often seemed content to draw with his peers. Bobby Fischer once gave him rope to hang himself by refusing a draw in an equal position.

FISCHER-PETROSIAN
Bled, 1961

196. Black moves
(a) Nxe4 (b) Rd6

(a) "Simply 1...Nxe4 leads to a dead draw" (Fischer). After 2.Rxe4 Rac8; 3.b3 Rd6 neither side can make serious progress.

Fischer wrote: "Black's solid as a rock and Petrosian offered a draw. I was ready to accept but Tal happened to be standing there at that instant, hovering anxiously since a drawn result would practically clinch first place for him. So I refused — not because I thought White has anything in the position, but because I didn't want to give Tal the satisfaction!"

(b) Petrosian, anxious to nail down the draw on the spot without facing the prospects of a long ending, played 1...Rd6? which proved to be his undoing. He overlooked 2.Bxa8 Rxd1+; 3.Kc2 Rf1; 4.Rxa5 Rxf2+; 5.Kb3 Rh2; 6.c5 Kd8; 7.Rb5! Rxh3; 8.Rb8+ Kc7; 9.Rb7+ Kc6; 10.Kc4 and Black resigns.

After 1...Rd6?; 2.Bxa8 Fischer notes: "This obvious capture shattered Petrosian, who apparently had been analyzing the intricacies of 2.Rxd6 Kxd6; 3.Rxe6+ fxe6; 4.Bxa8 Kc5; 5.b3 Nd7; 6.Kc2

Kd4 with an absolute bind on the dark squares."

Petrosian lost because he looked only for a way to force a quick draw. The excitement of struggling for the desired result blinded him once it seemed he had reached the goal. This fiasco illustrates Dr. Tarrasch's famous maxim: "When you don't know what to do wait for your opponent to get an idea — it's sure to be bad!"

DEMORALIZATION
When you start losing game after game, it's hard to keep up your spirits. Many of Fischer's opponents discovered this sad fact of life. Pundits dubbed it "Fischer fear."

TAIMANOV - FISCHER
5th match game, 1971

197. White moves
(a) Qf4+ (b) Rxf6

(a) Taimanov had already lost the first four games of this match. I was sitting in the audience when the players returned to finish this adjournment. I wondered why they even bothered to play it out since everyone expected an easy draw with 1.Qf4+ Qxf4; 2.Rxf4.

(b) With plenty of time on his clock a demoralized Taimanov snatched the tainted pawn and had to resign after 1.Rxf6?? Qd4+; 2.Rf2 Ra1+; 3.Kh2 Qxf2. Fischer, more surprised than anyone, shot me a smile to share his incredible good fortune.

He went on to win this match 6-0, then wiped out Larsen by the same score before beating Petrosian in the semi-finals that led to his victory over Spassky for the title in 1972.

Taimanov blamed his error on high blood pressure and a violent headache. "I never beat a healthy opponent," quipped Fischer.

WRONG WAY CORRIGAN
When players get excited and confused, they can forget even how the pieces move. This leads to all sorts of bizarre hallucinations.

GRINFELD - PANKINS
Kirov, 1974

198. White moves
(a) Qg3+ (b) h5

(a) White is two pawns up and should win. Instead he announced mate with 1.Qg3+. After 1...Kxg3 he realized too late that the pawn didn't guard the queen because it moved the other way!

(b) On 1.h5 Qf2+; 2.Qd2 Black runs out of good checks since now 2...Qf5+ (or 2...Qc5+; 3.Qc3+) 3.Qd3 forces an exchange of queens.

CHASING SHADOWS

When a player stands better throughout the game, it's hard to adjust to the fact that his advantage has evaporated. Here White makes an imprecise move yet continues to chase an illusion.

YERMOLINSKY - WOLFF
USA Championship, 1993

199. White moves
(a) Rb6 (b) Rb7

(a) White no longer stands better after 1.Rb7? Bd6! threatening a back rank mate. Play continued 2.f4 Kg8; 3.Qg4!? g6; 4.Qh4? (instead of settling for a draw by 4.Qxg6+! fxg6; 5.Rg7+ Kh8; 6.Rxg6+ Kh7; 7.Rg7+) 4...Bc5!; 5.Be5 c2; 6.Qxh6 Qxe3+; 7.Kh2 Qg1+ and White resigns.

(b) The significant difference is that White gets a big advantage by 1.Rb6! Bd6 (to stop Rxh6+) 2.f4 f6; 3.Rc6.

GARDEN VARIETY OVERSIGHTS

I was a safe pawn ahead with little to fear. All I had to do was consolidate and guard against White's only threat in the position. Ha!

KASHDAN - EVANS
USA Championship, 1948

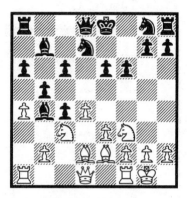

200. Black moves
(a) Nh6 (b) Qe7

(a) I was in too much of a hurry to castle and overlooked that White regains the pawn after 1...Nh6?; 2.Nxb5! Now 2...Bxd2 is refuted by 3.Nd6+ and Nxb7. White soon obtained the upper hand after 2...cxb5; 3.Bxb4 Kf7; 4.b3.

(b) 1...Qe7 is a solid way to meet the threat of Nxb5. If 2.e4 Nb6 holds everything. Also feasible is 1...c5!?

GIFT HORSES

After escaping from a bad position, many players are content to accept the offer of a draw without looking a gift horse in the mouth. Even world champions are susceptible to this kind of temptation.

LAUTIER - KASPAROV
Tilburg, 1997

201. Black moves
(a) c5 (b) Rd8

(a) Kasparov kicked himself for accepting a draw in the last round (which cost him clear first) instead of winning a pawn by 1...c5! The point is 2.bxc5? Rb8 picks up a piece in view of the back rank mate threat; or 2.Bc3 Rb8; 3.b5 Rxb5 snaring a pawn with excellent winning chances.

(b) Black makes no progress after 1...Rd8? 2.Kf1 giving White time to defend his weak back rank. The only rook move that makes sense is 1...Rb8; 2.Rxc6 Rxb4; 3.Rc2 Rxe4 which is hard to win because all the pawns are on the same side of the board.

CHANGING THE GUARD

It's easy to forget that every move alters the position. A piece that is defended one minute might no longer be defended the next minute. That's chess!

EVANS - WILLS
New Orleans, 1949

202. Black moves
(a) Bxf6 (b) Rxf6

(a) Black recaptured 1...Bxf6? forgetting that after 2.Nxc6 bxc6 his knight is no longer is guarded by the bishop on e7. Hence 3.Bxc5 caused him to resign.

(b) It's still a hard game after 1...Rxf6.

THE ULTIMATE FOLLY

Premature resignation is the ultimate folly. It's rare enough to capture headlines almost every time it happens between two grandmasters.

SVIDLER - LOBRON
Armenia Olympiad, 1996

203. Black moves
(a) f4 (b) Kg2

(a) This ending is deceptively simple. Black resigned because he thought 1...f4?; 2.Kc5! f3; 3.Kd4 f2; 4.Ke3 Kg2; 5.Ke2 is hopeless.

(b) Yet Black can salvage a draw by 1...Kg2!; 2.Kc5 h1/Q; 3.Rxh1 Kxh1; 4.Kd4 Kg2; 5.Ke5 Kf3!; 6.Kxf5 Ke3; 7.c4 Kd4 catching the pawn.

YOU CAN'T WIN BY RESIGNING

A month after Black resigned, an amateur discovered a hidden drawing resource. "If grandmasters can do things like that, there's still hope for me!" exclaimed one fan.

SHIROV - TIMMAN
Wijk aan Zee, 1996

204. Black moves
(a) Kd6 (b) Ke6

(a) The right defense is 1...Kd6!; 2.h4 Kxc6; 3.f5 Kd6! (in his mind's eye Timman probably only saw 3...gxf5?; 4.h5 Kd6; 5.g6 hxg6; 6.h6 and the pawn queens) 4.f6 Ke6; 5.Kf3 Kd6; 6.Ke4 Ke6; 7.Kd4 Kd6; 8.Kc4 Ke6; 9.Kc5 Kd7; 10.Kd5 Ke8!; 11.Kc6 Kd8; 12.f7 Ke7; 13.Kxc7 Kxf7; 14.Kd7 Kf8; 15.Ke6 Ke8; 16.Kf6 Kf8 and White can't make progress.

(b) Black can't afford to lose a tempo by 1...Ke6?; 2.h4! Kd5 (no better is 2...Kf5; 3.Kf3) 3.f5! gxf5; 4.h5 Ke6 (if 4...Ke5; 5.h6! f4; 6.g6 hxg6; 7.h7 wins) 5.Kf3 Ke5; 6.h6! does the trick.

SO-CALLED DEAD DRAWS

This game was adjourned and Black sealed a move. Several ki-
bitzers advised her not to bother playing out such an obviously
dead draw.

DREW - THOMPSON
British Ladies Championship, 1938

205. Black moves
(a) Qc7+ (b) Qc5+

(a) It's truly a dead draw after 1.Qc7+? Qb7.

(b) Black sealed 1...Qc5+! but then heeded the advice of vari-
ous spectators and informed her opponent she would be content with a draw. And so it was recorded. However, Black has a
forced mate with 2.Ka6 Qa3+; 3.Kb7 Qb4+; 4.Ka6 Qa4+; 5.Kb7
Qb5+; 6.Ka7 Kc7.

JUST PLAIN FATIGUE

"It's important to be rested when you sit down for a game. Unfortunately, the scheduling of games in many open tournaments — like this one, in which we had to play two games a day, makes that quite difficult," said Benko who finished his previous game at 4 a.m. and had to start this one at 10 in the morning.

BENKO - ROGERS
New York Open, 1990

206. White moves
(a) Nd1 (b) Nd5

(a) It's easy to see that Black must lose a piece after 1.Nd1! or even 1.Na2. So why didn't he play it?

Benko wrote: "Part of the reason was lack of sleep. I assumed without much calculation that moving my knight aggressively forward was better than the alternatives. It looks natural, doesn't it? I showed this position to three grandmasters and five masters, and asked each of them what move he would choose. Seven of them picked 1.Nd5 after a few moments' thought.

"That is not so amazing when you think about it. Chess is a vertical game. Pawns move only forward. We thus have a natural tendency to advance, and so we often do not give due consideration to moves that appear to be retreats. Tests have shown that we have little trouble seeing threats on the vertical plane, such as mate on the first rank, but we often miss horizontal threats."

(b) After 1.Nd5? Ne4; 2.Rxc4 (if 2.Qe1 Qd3 holds) 2...Nxd2; 3.Bxd2 cxd5; 4.Bxd5 Bxh3 they agreed to a draw.

BLUNDER OF THE YEAR
It's always news when a grandmaster walks into mate-in-one. How can such a thing happen without any prodding from the clock?

KARPOV - BAREEV
Linares, 1994

207. Black moves
(a) Rxd5 (b) Ba7

(a) A draw is likely after 1...Rxd5; 2.Nxd5 Ba7; 3.Ke2, etc.

(b) An amazing case of chess blindness occurred after 1...Ba7?? 2.Rxd8 mate. What probably happened is that instead of exchanging rooks, as planned, Black pictured the position after 1.Rxd5 Nxd5 in his mind's eye and assumed the rooks already were off the board. Alas, he got ahead of himself.

HANKY-PANKY?

Could any grandmaster worth his salt lose this ending after analyzing it overnight when the game was adjourned? Yet Black found a way to lose, prompting critics to accuse him of throwing the game. Was it carelessness or something more sinister?

KARPOV - POLUGAEVSKY
Tilburg, 1983

208. Black moves
(a) Kb4 (b) N6xa5

(a) It's hard to see how Black can lose after 1...Kb4; 2.Nc1 N6xa5; 3.Kxf4 Kc5; 4.Bxa5 Nxa5; 5.Kg5 Kd6; 6.Kg5 Ke7; 7.Kh6 Kf7.

(b) Black walked into a forced loss by 1...N/6xa5?; 2.Nxa5 Nxa5; 3.Bxa5 Kxa5; 4.Kxf4 Kb5; 5.Kg5 Kc5; 6.Kh6 Kd6; 7.Kxh7 Ke6; 8.Kg6 and the last pawn can't be stopped from queening.

Fischer once accused Soviets of throwing key games to each other in international tourneys. GM Yasser Seirawan, when asked if he ever saw any evidence of this in his own experience, said: "His charge is absolutely true! I've seen it happen. Soviet stars knew they were expected to finish behind Karpov and I saw Polugaevsky throw away an easy draw against him in this simple endgame. When Spassky committed the crime of finishing first ahead of Karpov in Spain, they cut off his interzonal funding — which is why Spassky left Russia and went to play for France in the Olympiads."

PLAYING TO LOSE

Black is an exchange and three pawns ahead. His position is so strong that it's almost impossible to find a bad move.

GARCIA - IVKOV
Havana, 1965

209. Black moves
(a) d3 (b) Qd1

(a) Black found just about the only losing move with 1...d3??; 2.Bc3 followed by Qh8 mate. This error, unlike most of the others cited in this book, was caused by extreme time pressure.

(b) It's hard to see how White can survive much longer after 1...Qd1; 2.Bh6 Rb8 threatening Qxf1+ followed by Rb1.

ASLEEP AT THE SWITCH
Some mistakes go unnoticed because neither side is aware that the position contains a hidden resource. Such oversights are usually caused by lack of skill, but consider this example between two grandmasters who should know better.

SHABALOV - KUDRIN
USA Championship, 1997

210. Black moves
(a) Rc8 (b) Bxc3

(a) Material is even but Black missed a great opportunity and eventually lost after 1...Rc8?; 2 Ne4.

(b) Neither player suspected that Black can win two pawns by 1...Bxc3!; 2.bxc3 Bxc2+!; 3.Kxc2 Rxa2+ regaining the piece with interest (if 4.Kd3 Nde5+; 5.Ke4 Rxe2). This oversight was probably caused by Black's reluctance to part with the two bishops.

DECEPTIVE SIMPLICITY

Many players tend to relax when complications are over and the smoke has cleared. But you can't afford to let your guard down just because things look simple.

GELLER-FISCHER
Mallorca, 1970

211. White moves
(a) Kg3 (b) Rd2

(a) Although a pawn down, White can achieve an easy book draw by 1.Kg3! Kg5; 2.Rd5.

(b) Instead Geller carelessly played 1.Rd2? Kh4; 2.Kxf5 g3. He thought this move could be answered by the illegal 3.fxg3+ — a strange hallucination. Both sides were shaken by the turn of events and the game continued: 3.f4 Kh3? (stronger is Ra1) 4.Rd3 Kh4 (if 4...Kh2; 5.Kg4 g2; 6.Rh3+ Kg1; 7.f5 Kf2; 8.Rh2 draws) 5.Rd2? (the correct drawing line is 5.Rd8!) 5...Ra1; 6.Ke5?? (the final indignity; 6.Rd8! g2; 7.Rh8+ Kf3; 8.Ke6! still draws) 6...Kg4; 7.f5 Ra5+. White resigns.

DOUBLE CHECK
In this unusual position White's king is checked by both a rook and pawn. He failed to find an escape hatch and resigned.

NEPOMUSENA - PALASIOS
Brazil, 1971

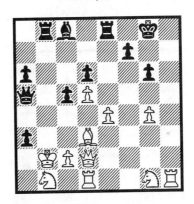

212. White moves
(a) Kc1 (b) Ka1

(a) Hopeless is 1.Kc1? Rxb1+!; 2.Kxb1 Qb6+; 3.Ka1 Qb2 mate.

(b) Assuming that the same fate awaited him after 1.Ka1 Rxb1+ and seeing no way out of his predicament, White gave up. But he can draw by refusing to take the rook! The correct defense is 1.Ka1! Rxb1+; 2.Ka2! Black, still a piece down, now has nothing better than to go for perpetual check by 2...Rb2+; 3.Ka1 Rb1+ (but not 3...Qb6?; 4.Qc3) 4.Ka2, etc.

ANOTHER OPTICAL ILLUSION

In the 1930s players trembled before Czech grandmaster Salo Flohr, who was a giant of the chess world. Here, however, he stumbled against Henri Grob, a famous Swiss portrait painter, by failing to find a defense to the threat of Qf1 mate.

FLOHR - GROB
1st match game, 1933

213. White moves
(a) Qe1 (b) Kh1

(a) Flohr resigned in a winning position because he saw nothing better than 1.Qe1? Qxd5 gaining a piece with mate looming on g2. .

(b) White's extra pawn should prove decisive after 1.Kh1! Qf1+ (if 1...Qxb2; 2.Qe8+ Kh7; 3.Bxf7) 2.Bg1. This simple defense eluded him.

TRUSTING HIM

According to published reports, Soviet champion Leonid Stein was not in time pressure when he lavished over 20 minutes on his next lemon. Emma's response was equally amazing.

EMMA - STEIN
Mar del Plata, 1966

214. Black moves
(a) Bc8 (b) Qc2

(a) Although an exchange down, Black has excellent winning chances with 1...Bc8 intending Bh3+.

(b) Stein rejected perpetual check by 1...Qh3+; 2.Kf2 Qh2+ and got too wound up looking for a forced win. Concentrating intensely, he put his queen en prise with 1...Qc2?? Now 2.Nxc2 would have prompted his immediate resignation but White could not bring himself to believe that his renowned opponent could make such a blunder after so much thought. Emma trusted Stein and, almost in a reflex gesture, defended his rook by 2.Rd7? The game was drawn 14 moves later after this astounding double error.

THE CLOCK FORCES ERROR

This concluding example features the kind of time pressure antics excluded from this collection because anything can happen when a player has to move fast just to reach the time control.

RESHEVSKY - SAVON
Petropolis, 1973

215. White moves
(a) Qxg6+ (b) Rh8+

(a) White announced mate with 1.Qxg6+?? but forgot about the bishop lurking on b1 far removed from the scene of action. Out of sight, out of mind.

(b) With more time Reshevsky surely would have found a forced mate with 1.Rh8+ Kg5; 2.h4+ Kxh4; 3.Rxh5+ gxh5; 4.Qxh5.

Every example cited in this book was conducted at a time limit of 40 moves in 2 hours or slower. As time controls accelerate, in an attempt to make chess a popular spectator sport, mistakes forced by the clock will become ever more commonplace. Expect chess of the future to reflect the price paid for speed.

Chapter 11

ANATOMY OF AN ERROR

*"The greatest blunders, like the thickest ropes, are often compounded
of a multitude of strands. Take the rope apart, separate it into the
small threads that compose it, and you can break them one by one."*
— Victor Hugo

The first move in chess is akin to the serve in tennis. White
enjoys an initiative and wins the majority of games, yet nobody
has ever been able to prove there is a forced win. Even if computers solve the mystery of chess, which appears likely, it still
won't destroy the popularity of our ancient pastime.

It's axiomatic that the starting lineup is drawn with best play.
Like tic-tac-toe. But not all draws are perfect. Since there are a
dozen ways to go wrong at every turn, draws frequently are the
product of mistakes that cancel each other out.

Unlike cards or other games of chance, chess is decided by the
failings of one of the players. Win, lose, or draw — you have
nobody to blame but yourself. You can't win unless your opponent errs; and you can't lose unless you err. Skill, in fact, might
be defined as the ability to exploit the other guy's mistake.

DESTRUCTIVE HABITS

The following plea from an avid chess student appeared over the Internet:

"I'm an experienced beginner rated about 1200. I've studied openings enough to know the most common lines resulting from what I will do as White and Black. So far it hasn't been much to worry about. The bulk of my study at the moment is tactical, and I also devote a few hours every week to endgames. I'm pleased with my progress so far, as I can easily measure it comparing records of games I played several months ago with recent ones. In other words, I think I'm studying correctly.

"My problem is I'm having a terrible time with blunders in rated games. I don't mean miscalculations or misjudgments. I mean just horrible mistakes. The sort that severely cripple my game against an equal or better opponent.

"Last week against a 1650 player I gave away a bishop on the fifth move! No material compensation, no space compensation, no tempo gain, no nothing. I mean, two question marks wasn't nearly strong enough to describe this lemon. I tried my damnedest to salvage the game but it was already over and I finally resigned on the 18th move.

"Last night I played an opponent who is slightly stronger, rated about 1270. I fought hard for the initiative (I was Black) and stood well in the early middle game. Then I blundered and lost the exchange (rook for bishop). My pawn structure was still superior, so I felt pretty good about my chances to fight back. I did. We reached an even endgame. Naturally, I felt pretty good about my chances again. Then I gave away a knight (sigh). Not in time trouble at all. In fact, he was. I resigned on the 35th move.

"Needless to say, I'm quite frustrated. I don't mind getting outplayed and losing. In fact, I relish it because I like to see what he did better than I did. However, I lost both these games thanks to my own stupidity. Truth be told, I'd probably have lost the first one anyway after making him work for 30 or 40 moves, but I'm sure I could have won last night.

"So, I wind up going home. Rather than examining my losses and looking for mistakes, I just grumble about how stupid I was. I'd like to solve the problem. My feeling is that I lack some kind of basic discipline but that it's possible to develop more patience. Does anyone remember a similar point in their own chess development?"

ATTITUDE ADJUSTMENT

If his problem sounds familiar, then you need an attitude adjustment. After deciding on a move, say to yourself, "I'm human and I know I blunder all too often. Is this the move that's going to ruin my day?"

In other words, assume your move is a blunder until you check it out carefully. Don't just look at what you threaten – look at what threatens you!

Does this mean you have to spend the rest of your chess life searching for silly mistakes after every move? Yes, but with practice it will become second nature. To some extent even masters must be on the prowl for dumb mistakes.

I found it hard to handle chords when I was learning to play the piano. Sometimes my fingers hurt. I asked a friend who was an accomplished musician how he did it and he showed me how he positioned his fingers. "Now it doesn't matter what position my fingers are in — it just got easier somehow," he said. His words reminded me of how Bobby Fischer explained his great leap in chess ability. "One day I just got good," he said.

I joined the Marshall Club in Manhattan at age 12. One day, after losing to an expert, he reviewed the game with me and praised some of my moves. "The game was even until you blundered away a piece, then it was over," he said. "All you need to do to improve is avoid obvious mistakes."

Maybe it's not "romantic" to think that avoiding mistakes is the way to improve, but a certain maturity makes for better chess. It's far more important to avoid doing anything stupid than to create brilliant combinations. Progress in tactical ability won't matter all that much until you take care of those blunders.

In searching for the anatomy of an error our most important tool is retrograde analysis. We must work backwards, one move at a time, examining each new position under a microscope. Masters use this method when brewing opening innovations in their secret workshops. It's called home cooking.

For example, I ran across this diagram where Black unleashed a bolt from the blue.

CAN BLACK PIERCE THE WALL?

Black's attack appears to have come to a standstill. Unless he finds a way to breach the pawn barrier on the kingside, he will be forced to retrench. It's now or never!

216. Black moves

The finale featured a stunning queen sacrifice: 1...Bh3!!; 2.bxc7? Bxg2+!; 3.Kxg2 Qh3+!!; 4.Kxh3 Ng5+; 5.Kg2 Nh4+; 6.Kh1 g2 mate. (Note that diagram 216 is a position after 22.Bg1 in the following game.)

It's hard to believe that White is really lost after 1...Bh3! Clearly he must find something better than 2.bxc7 which could be branded the losing move. My first try was 2.Re1 but I saw this is crushed by 2...Bxg2+! 3.Kxg2 Qh3+!! (anyway) 4.Kxh3 Ng5+; 5.Kg2 Nh4+; 6.Kf1 g2+; 7.Kf2 Nh3 mate. The hapless king is smothered by his own men. The only way to survive is to give up the exchange by 2.gxh3 Qxh3; 3.Rf2 gxf2; 4.Bxf2 and White must fight for a draw.

Where did White go wrong and how far back must we go to find it in a post-mortem? To answer this question we have to look at the body of the game and perform a classic autopsy.

Now let's take a look at the whole game from the start.

GM LUBOMIR FTACNIK - GM OGNJEN CVITAN
King's Indian Defense, Germany, 1997

1.d4 Nf6; 2.Nf3 g6; 3.c4 Bg7; 4.Nc3 0-0; 5.e4 d6; 6.Be2 e5; 7.0-0 Nc6; 8.d5 Ne7.

217. Position after 8...Ne7

This position has been reached thousands of times in master games. Who stands better? Probably the better player!

9.Nd2 Ne8; 10.b4 f5; 11.c5 Nf6; 12.f3 f4; 13.Nc4 g5; 14.a4 Ng6; 15.Ba3 Rf7; 16.b5 dxc5; 17.Bxc5 h5; 18.a5 g4; 19.b6 g3; 20.Kh1 Nh7; 21.d6 Qh4; 22.Bg1 Bh3; 23.bxc7 Bxg2; 24.Kxg2 Qh3; 25.Kxh3 Ng5; 26.Kg2 Nh4; 27.Kh1 g2 mate.

The task is to find where White missed his last chance to control the game before 22...Bh3. Can you identify the culprit?

We can safely rule out the first 15 moves which have been tested many times in recent years and are now fairly routine. Both sides are racing to attack on opposite wings and current theory holds that White keeps the edge once he safeguards his king, which is easier said than done.

Since White stands worse after 22...Bh3! his fatal error must have come between a narrow window from moves 16-21. Let's start with the position just before diagram 216 (after 20...Nh7).

218. White moves

Fortunately we don't have to go back very far in this little detective story. The plausible 21.d6? is the miscreant because it sets White up for Black's ensuing combination. If White saw what was coming, what could he do to stop it?

One solution is the quiet 21.Re1! in order to vacate f1 for the bishop, putting an end to all those nasty threats against g2. If 21...axb6; 22.axb6 Rxa1; 23.Qxa1 Qh4 (or 23...h4; 24.h3 Bxh3; 24.gxh3 Qd7; 25.Bf1) 24.Bg1 Bh3?; 25.Bf1! repulses the attack and leaves Black vulnerable on the queenside. Better is 21...cxb6; 22.axb6 a6 with a hard struggle in the offing.

In reviewing decisive games for my weekly syndicated newspaper column I usually try to pinpoint the losing moves. Solving this task is not only fun but also one of the best ways to improve our own game. Simply take the rope apart and separate it into small threads.

INDEX OF PLAYERS

(Numbers refer to diagrams)

KASPAROV CHESS GK2100™
SAITEK - The World Leader in Intelligent Electronic Games

THE BEST VALUE MONEY CAN BUY! - The **fabulous** Kasparov GK2100 is the **most popular** chess computer we sell. Using a super high speed **RISC** computer chip and rated at a **2334** USCF rating, you'll have consistent challenges and excitement. Coaching features and fun levels makes it suitable for novices; masters and experts will want to choose higher levels.

GREAT DESIGN - Packaged in a sleek, handsome cabinet suitable for your living room. No need to find a partner to play - **take on the Champion**!

POWERFUL PROGRAM FEATURES - **64 levels of play** include sudden death, tournament, problem solving and beginner's. Shows intended move and position evaluation, take back up to 50 moves, and user selectable **book openings library**. Also choose from **Active**, **Passive**, **Tournament, complete book, no book**. Select the high speed **Selective Search** or play against the powerful **Brute Force.** program. Thinks in opponents time for best realism. Shutoff, shut on memory - remembers game for 1 year!

GREAT FOR BEGINNERS AND MASTERS ALIKE! - This **awesome program** can beat over 99% of all regular chess players, yet it is still suitable for beginners and intermediate players: Simply set the skill level to the appropriate strength for the best challenges. Matching your skill to the correct level of play ensures a **challenging** and **exciting** game.

EVEN MORE FEATURES - Opening library of 35,000 moves, **large LCD** shows full information and keeps track of playing time. Modern ergonomic design goes well in living room.

To order, send $199.95 for the <u>Kasparov Chess GK2100</u>

CARDOZA PUBLISHING CHESS BOOKS

- OPENINGS -

WINNING CHESS OPENINGS by Bill Robertie - Shows concepts and best opening moves of more than 25 essential openings from Black's and White's perspectives: King's Gambit, Center Game, Scotch Game, Giucco Piano, Vienna Game, Bishop's Opening, Ruy Lopez, French, Caro-Kann, Sicilian, Alekhine, Pirc, Modern, Queen's Gambit, Nimzo-Indian, Queen's Indian, Dutch, King's Indian, Benoni, English, Bird's, Reti's, and King's Indian Attack. Examples from 25 grandmasters and champions including Fischer and Kasparov. 144 pages, $9.95

WORLD CHAMPION OPENINGS by Eric Schiller - This serious reference work covers the essential opening theory and moves of every major chess opening and variation as played by all the world champions. Reading as much like an encyclopedia of the must-know openings crucial to every chess player's knowledge as a powerful tool showing the insights, concepts and secrets as used by the greatest players of all time, World Champion Openings (WCO) covers an astounding 100 crucial openings in full conceptual detail (with 100 actual games from the champions themselves)! A must-have book for serious chess players. 384 pages, $18.95

STANDARD CHESS OPENINGS by Eric Schiller - The new definitive standard on opening chess play in the 20th century, this comprehensive guide covers every important chess opening and variation ever played and currently in vogue. In all, more than 3,000 opening strategies are presented! Differing from previous opening books which rely almost exclusively on bare notation, SCO features substantial discussion and analysis on each opening so that you learn and understand the concepts behind them. Includes more than 250 completely annotated games (including a game representative of each major opening) and more than 1,000 diagrams! For modern players at any level, this is the standard reference book necessary for competitive play. A must have for serious chess players!!! 768 pages, $24.95

UNORTHODOX CHESS OPENINGS by Eric Schiller - The exciting guide to all the major unorthodox openings used by chess players, contains more than 1,500 weird, contentious, controversial, unconventional, arrogant, and outright strange opening strategies. From their tricky tactical surprises to their bizarre names, these openings fly in the face of tradition. You'll meet such openings as the Orangutang, Raptor Variation, Halloween Gambit, Double Duck, Frankenstein-Dracula Variation, and even the Drunken King! These openings are a sexy and exotic way to spice up a game and a great weapon to spring on unsuspecting and often unprepared opponents. More than 750 diagrams show essential positions. 528 pages, $24.95

GAMBIT OPENING REPERTOIRE FOR WHITE by Eric Schiller - Chessplayers who enjoy attacking from the very first move are rewarded here with a powerful repertoire of brilliant gambits. Starting off with 1.e4 or 1.d4 and then using such sharp weapons such as the Göring Gambit (Accepted and Declined), Halasz Gambit, Alapin Gambit, Ulysses Gambit, Short Attack and many more, to put great pressure on opponents, Schiller presents a complete attacking repertoire to use against the most popular defenses, including the Sicilian, French, Scandinavian, Caro-Kann, Pirc, Alekhine, and other Open Game positions. 192 pages, $14.95.

GAMBIT OPENING REPERTOIRE FOR BLACK by Eric Schiller - For players that like exciting no-holds-barred chess, this versatile gambit repertoire shows Black how to take charge with aggressive attacking defenses against any orthodox first White opening move; 1.e4, 1.d4 and 1.c4. Learn the Scandinavian Gambit against 1.e4, the Schara Gambit and Queen's Gambit Declined variations against 1.d4, and some flank and unorthodox gambits also. Black learns the secrets of seizing the initiative from White's hands, usually by investing a pawn or two, to begin powerful attacks that can send White to early defeat. 176 pages, $14.95.

COMPLETE DEFENSE TO QUEEN PAWN OPENINGS by Eric Schiller - This aggressive counterattacking repertoire covers Black opening systems against virtually every chess opening except for 1.e4 (including most flank games), based on the exciting and powerful Tarrasch Defense, an opening that helped bring Championship titles to Kasparov and Spassky. Black learns to effectively use the Classical Tarrasch, Symmetrical Tarrasch, Asymmetrical Tarrasch, Marshall and Tarrasch Gambits, and Tarrasch without Nc3, to achieve an early equality or even an outright advantage in the first few moves. 288 pages, $16.95.

COMPLETE DEFENSE TO KING PAWN OPENINGS by *Eric Schiller* - Learn a complete defensive system against 1.e4. This powerful repertoire not only limits White's ability to obtain any significant opening advantage but allows Black to adopt the flexible Caro-Kann formation, the favorite weapon of many of the greatest chess players. All White's options are explained in detail, and a plan is given for Black to combat them all. Analysis is up-to-date and backed by examples drawn from games of top stars. Detailed index lets you follow the opening from the point of a specific player, or through its history. 240 pages, $16.95.

SECRETS OF THE SICILIAN DRAGON by *GM Eduard Gufeld and Eric Schiller* - The mighty Dragon Variation of the Sicilian Defense is one of the most exciting openings in chess. Everything from opening piece formation to the endgame, including clear explanations of all the key strategic and tactical ideas, is covered in full conceptual detail. Instead of memorizing a jungle of variations, you learn the really important ideas behind the opening, and how to adapt them at the chessboard. Special sections on the heroes of the Dragon show how the greatest players handle the opening. The most instructive book on the Dragon written! 208 pages, $14.95.

- MIDDLEGAME/TACTICS/WINNING CONCEPTS -

10 MOST COMMON CHESS MISTAKES, and How to Fix Them by *Larry Evans* - A fascinating collection of more than 200 typical errors committed by the world's greatest players challenges readers to test their skills by choosing between two moves, the right one, or the one actually played. Readers will be amazed at how even world champions stumble by violating basic principles. From neglecting development, king safety, misjudging threats, premature attacks, to impulsiveness, snatching pawns, and basic inattention, readers get a complete course in exactly where they can go wrong and how to fix their game. 256 pages, $14.95.

WORLD CHAMPION COMBINATIONS by *Keene and Schiller* - Learn the insights, concepts and moves of the greatest combinations ever by the greatest players who ever lived. From Morphy to Alekhine, to Fischer to Kasparov, the incredible combinations and brilliant sacrifices of the 13 World Champions are collected here in the most insightful combinations book written. Packed with fascinating strategems, 50 annotated games, and great practical advice for your own games, this is a great companion guide to *World Champion Openings*. 264 pages, $16.95.

WINNING CHESS TACTICS by *Bill Robertie* - 14 chapters of winning tactical concepts show the complete explanations and thinking behind every tactical concept: pins, single and double forks, double attacks, skewers, discovered and double checks, multiple threats - and other crushing tactics to gain an immediate edge over opponents. Learn the power tools of tactical play to become a stronger player. Includes guide to chess notation. 128 pages, $9.95

ENCYCLOPEDIA OF CHESS WISDOM, The Essential Concepts and Strategies of Smart Chess Play by *Eric Schiller* - The most important concepts, strategies, tactics, wisdom, and thinking that every chessplayer must know, plus the gold nuggets of knowledge behind every attack and defense, is collected together in one highly focused volume. From opening, middle and endgame strategy, to psychological warfare and tournament tactics, the *Encyclopedia of Chess Wisdom* forms the blueprint of power play and advantage at the chess board. Step-by-step, the reader is taken through the thinking behind each essential concept, and through examples, discussions, and diagrams, shown the full impact on the game's direction. You even learn how to correctly study chess to become a chess master. 400 pages, $19.95.

- BEGINNING CHESS BOOKS -

THE BASICS OF WINNING CHESS by *Jacob Cantrell* - A great first book of chess, in one easy reading, beginner's learn the moves of the pieces, the basic rules and principles of play, the standard openings, and both Algebraic and English chess notation. The basic ideas of the winning concepts and strategies of middle and end game play are shown as well. Includes example games of great champions. 64 pages, $4.95.

BEGINNING CHESS PLAY by *Bill Robertie* - Step-by-step approach uses 113 diagrams to teach novices the basic principles of chess. Covers opening, middle and end game strategies, principles of development, pawn structure, checkmates, openings and defenses, how to write and read chess notation, join a chess club, play in tournaments, use a chess clock, and get rated. Two annotated games illlustrate strategic thinking for easy learning. 144 pages, $9.95

WHIZ KIDS TEACH CHESS *Edited by Eric Schiller* - Ten of today's greatest young stars, ranging from 10-17 years old–some perhaps to be future world champions–present a fascinating look on learning chess. Each tells of their successes, failures, world travels, and love of the game, show off their best moves, and even admit to their most embarrassing blunders. At the heart of this inspirational book targeted toward beginning, under-17 players, is a basic chess primer with large diagrams, clear explanations, and winning ideas. Features Jordy Mont-Reynaud (14), who smashed Bobby Fischer's record by over two years to become the youngest USCF Master, Vinay Bhat (12), Gabe Kahane (16), the Karnazes' twins (10), Irina Krush (15), Asuka Nakamura (11), Hikaru Nakamura (10), and Jennifer Shahade (16). 128 large format pages, $14.95.

- MATES & ENDGAMES -

303 TRICKY CHECKMATES *by Fred Wilson and Bruce Alberston* - Both a fascinating challenge and great training tool, this collection of two, three and bonus four move checkmates is great for advanced beginning, intermediate and expert players. Mates are in order of difficulty, from the simple to very complex positions. Learn the standard patterns and stratagems for cornering the king: corridor and support mates, attraction and deflection sacrifices, pins and annihilation, the quiet move, and the dreaded *zugzwang*. Examples, drawn from actual games, illustrate a wide range of chess tactics from old classics right up to the 1990's. 192 pages, $12.95.

MASTER CHECKMATE STRATEGY *by Bill Robertie* - Learn the basic combinations, plus advanced, surprising and unconventional mates, the most effective pieces needed to win, and how to mate opponents with just a pawn advantage. also, how to work two rooks into an unstoppable attack; how to wield a queen advantage with deadly intent; how to coordinate pieces of differing strengths into indefensible positions of their opponents; when it's best to have a knight, and when a bishop to win. 144 pages, $9.95

BASIC ENDGAME STRATEGY: Kings, Pawns and Minor Pieces *by Bill Robertie* - Learn the mating principles and combinations needed to finish off opponents. From the four basic checkmates using the King with the queen, rook, two bishops, and bishop/knight combinations, to the King/pawn, King/Knight and King/Bishop endgames, you'll learn the essentials of translating small edges into decisive checkmates. Learn the 50-move rule, and the combinations of pieces that can't force a mate against a lone King. 144 pages, $12.95.

BASIC ENDGAME STRATEGY: Rooks and Queens by Bill Robertie - The companion guide to *Basic Endgame Strategy: Kings, Pawns and Minor Pieces*, you'll learn the basic mating principles and combinations of the Queen and Rook with King, how to turn middlegame advantages into victories, by creating passed pawns, using the King as a weapon, clearing the way for rook mates, and other endgame combinations. 144 pages, $12.95.

EXCELLENT CHESS BOOKS - OTHER PUBLISHERS

- OPENINGS -

HOW TO PLAY THE TORRE *by Eric Schiller* - One of Schiller's best-selling books, the 19 chapters on this fabulous and aggressive White opening (1. d4 Nf6; 2. Nf3 e6; 3. Bg5) will make opponents shudder and get you excited about chess all over again. Insightful analysis, completely annotated games get you ready to win! 210 pages, $17.50.

A BLACK DEFENSIVE SYSTEM WITH 1...D6 *by Andrew Soltis* - This Black reply - so rarely played that it doesn't even have a name - throws many opponents off their rote attack and can lead to a decisive positional advantage. Use this surprisingly strong system to give you the edge against unprepared opponents. 166 pages, $16.50.

BLACK TO PLAY CLASSICAL DEFENSES AND WIN *by Eric Schiller* - Shows you how to develop a complete opening repertoire as black. Emerge from *any* opening with a playable position, fighting for the center from the very first move. Defend against the Ruy Lopez, Italian Game, King's Gambit, King's Indian, many more. 166 pages, $16.50.

ROMANTIC KING'S GAMBIT IN GAMES & ANALYSIS *by Santasiere & Smith* - The most comprehensive collection of theory and games (137) on this adventurous opening is filled with annotations and "color" on the greatest King's Gambits played and the players. Makes you *want* to play! Very readable; packed with great concepts. 233 pages, $17.50.

WHITE TO PLAY 1.E4 AND WIN by Eric Schiller - Shows you how to develop a complete opening system as white beginning 1. e4. Learn the recommended opening lines to all the major systems as white, and how to handle any defense black throws back. Covers the Sicilian, French, Caro-Kann, Scandinavia; many more. 166 pages, $16.50.

MIDDLEGAME/TACTICS/WINNING CONCEPTS -

CHESS TACTICS FOR ADVANCED PLAYERS by Yuri Averbakh - A great tactical book. Complex combinations are brilliantly simpified into basic, easy-to-understand concepts you can use to win. Learn the underlying structure of piece harmony and fortify skills through numerous exercises. Very instructive, a must read. 328 pages, $17.50.

STRATEGY FOR ADVANCED PLAYERS by Eric Schiller - For intermediate to advanced players, 45 insightful and very informative lessons illustrate the strategic and positional factors you need to know in middle and endgame play. Recommended highly as a tool to learn strategic chess and become a better player. 135 pages, $14.50.

- ENDGAMES -

ESSENTIAL CHESS ENDINGS EXPLAINED VOL. 1 by Jeremy Silman - This essential and enjoyable reference tool to mates and stalemates belongs in every chess player's library. Commentary on every move plus quizzes and many diagrams insure complete understanding. All basic positions covered, plus many advanced ones. 221 pages, $16.50.

ESSENTIAL CHESS ENDINGS EXPLAINED VOL. 2 by Ken Smith - This book assumes you know the basics of the 1st volume and takes you all the way to Master levels. Work through moves of 275 positions and learn as you go. There are explanations of every White and Black move so you know what's happening from both sides. 298 pages, $17.50.